How to Pass
Practical
Word Processing

FIRST, SECOND AND THIRD LEVELS

Pam Smith

BA Hons PGCE

London Chamber of Commerce and Industry Examinations Board
Athena House
112 Station Road
Sidcup
Kent DA15 7BJ
United Kingdom

First published 1999
Reprinted 2001

British Library Cataloguing-in-Publication Data
Smith, Pam
   How to pass practical word processing : first, second and third levels
   1.Word processing – Examinations – Study guides
   I. Title
   652.5

ISBN 1 86247 095 2

10   9   8   7   6   5   4   3   2

Typeset by the London Chamber of Commerce
and Industry Examinations Board
Printed in Great Britain by Henry Ling Ltd.,
at the Dorset Press, Dorchester, Dorset.
Reprinted in Great Britain by Multiplex Techniques Ltd.,
Brook Industrial Park, Mill Brook Road, St. Mary Cray, Kent. BR5 3TX

Contents

Contents

About the author

Pam Smith is currently a Lecturer in the School of Information Processing at North West Kent College in Dartford. She has also taught in colleges in Bournemouth, Bristol and Hertfordshire. A linguist by training, she has over 20 years' experience of teaching in England and Spain. She now teaches secretarial skills, information technology and languages to students of all ages.

Pam is Chief Examiner in Practical Word Processing for the LCCIEB and has been closely involved in the development of the practical assessment schemes. She is also a Chief Examiner for two other examinations boards.

Introduction

In today's computerised workplace, proven ability in word processing has become a basic requirement for the majority of employees. Such skill is highly regarded and sought by employers and most job advertisements include word processing as an essential skill.

A highly regarded qualification in word processing is proof of such skill, and the LCCI Examinations Board offers Practical Word Processing assignments at three levels to enable candidates to gain a formal qualification as evidence of their word-processing skills.

Objective

This book is designed to help candidates preparing for the LCCI Examinations Board assignments in Practical Word Processing at **First**, **Second** and **Third Levels**.

After working through the exercises contained in this book, candidates should be able to approach the assignments with confidence.

The Practical Word Processing scheme

The aim of the Practical Word Processing scheme is to assess the candidate's practical ability across the key word processing areas of:

- file handling and management
- file editing and formatting
- multi-page documents and multiple document creation and handling
- technically complex document creation
- mail merge.

The target audience for the scheme includes those who are:

- wishing to acquire the fundamental practical word-processing skills for modern business
- starting a career in industry and need the word-processing skills to support that career
- returning to work or business and need to update their word-processing skill base
- requiring an expanded skill set for job enhancement or promotion.

Format of assignments

At each level, a set of six assignments is designed to test the candidate's skill in a range of functional areas. Each assignment is given an individual time allowance ranging from 30 minutes at **First Level** to a maximum of 60 minutes at **Second** and **Third Levels**.

The assignments are designed to be taken when the candidate and the tutor agree that the candidate possesses the necessary skill to complete the assignment to a satisfactory standard. In this way, the candidate can progress at his or her own pace, irrespective of the rest of the group.

All assignments are marked and graded by the tutor and sent for moderation to the LCCI Examinations Board.

The scheme is available on demand, which means it is perfect for courses of study which do not necessarily fall within the standard academic calendar for testing.

Syllabus functions

First Level

First Level assignments will test the candidate's ability to perform the following functions:

1 Create and save a file
2 Retrieve and open a file
3 Enter text to create a document
4 Edit text
5 Enhance text
6 Format and amend the layout of a document
7 Use standard manuscript corrections
8 Recognise errors and perform corrections
9 Print a document

Only when the candidate has demonstrated skill in the above functions should the assignments be attempted. Each assignment at **First Level** has a time allowance of 30 minutes.

Second Level

Second Level assignments test a further range of skills, based on the candidate's progression towards longer and more complicated documents. All functions at **First Level** may be tested with the addition of the following:

1 Advanced formatting
2 Search and replace
3 Headers and footers
4 Simple pagination of documents
5 Block functions
6 Mail merge
7 Boilerplating (creating and using standard paragraphs)
8 Simple table functions
9 Rearrangement of text in a specified order
10 Form design

11 Expansion of abbreviations

12 An instruction given once but expected to apply throughout a document

13 Leaving space of specified size (vertically and horizontally)

14 Entering documents from manuscript

At **Second Level**, all but one assignment (Assignment 6) has a time allowance of 60 minutes. Assignments 4 and 5 consist of two parts, each part taking 30 minutes for completion. Many of the assignments are handwritten.

Third Level

The **Third Level** assignments demand even greater skill and test the following functions:

1 Graphic handling

2 Paper size and orientation

3 Font styles and sizes, special characters

4 Complex tables

5 Boxes, borders and shading

6 Multi-level paragraph numbering

7 Advanced page numbering

8 Advanced formatting

9 Reorganisation of information

10 Footnotes

11 Column facilities

12 Advanced printing facilities

13 Moving text blocks between files and inserting text files in documents

14 Standard and non-standard manuscript correction signs

15 Inconsistencies of layout within a document

Third Level assignments are given a time allowance of 45 minutes (Assignments 1 and 6) or 60 minutes (Assignments 2–5). Most of the assignments are handwritten.

How to use this workbook

Before using this book, candidates should already have a basic keyboarding ability and be able to perform basic word-processing functions. They should also have developed good proofreading and error-correction skills.

This book will enable candidates for each of the three levels of Practical Word Processing assignments to check what is required for each level and practise the functions which will later be tested under examination conditions.

1

The basics

After carefully studying this chapter, you should be able to:

1 *recognise the need for sensible use of your time;*

2 *recognise the procedures involved in creating, saving and retrieving files;*

3 *identify the kinds of text amendment you will need to undertake;*

4 *identify the correction signs and abbreviations that may be used;*

5 *identify the need for attractive display and careful proofreading;*

6 *check your skill in practice exercises.*

Extended Syllabus references

First Level

Candidates must be able to:

1.1 Create a new file

1.2 Save new file

1.3 Store new file on disk

1.4 Save (store) retrieved file under a different file name

2.1 Retrieve and open a file created and saved (stored) by self

2.2 Retrieve and open a file created and saved (stored) by another

Note: Simple access file names and locations should be specified

3.1 Enter text from simple typescript using default margins and layout

Note: Text to be entered should contain standard alphabet, numeric and punctuation characters. The vocabulary should be standard with no specialised technical terms

4.1 Insert text, characters, words, phrases and lines of text

4.2 Delete text, characters, words, phrases and lines of text

4.3 Add a line space between items

4.4 Delete a line space between items

Note: Text to be edited should contain standard alphabet, numeric and punctuation characters. The vocabulary should be standard with no specialised technical terms

(continued)

Extended Syllabus references (continued)

7.1   Use the standard manuscript corrections in Appendix A when entering or editing text

8.1   Proofread document and make corrections

8.2   Use spellchecker to check document and make corrections

9.1   Print document from screen

Note: Print should be one copy of document on A4 paper.

9.2   Check printed document

9.3   Edit text to produce correct print-out

Second Level

Candidates must be able to:

11.1   Expand in full abbreviations listed in Appendix B when entering or editing text

Note: Abbreviations may not be included within the assignments at First Level

12.1   Extend instruction relating to formatting

12.2   Extend instruction relating to headers/footers

12.3   Extend instruction relating to page numbering

12.4   Extend instruction relating to search and replace

12.5   Extend implied inclusion of 'Enc' in letters

14.1   Enter documents from manuscript, typescript or mixture of both

Note: The text may contain more complex vocabulary than First Level, eg more place names and simple technical words and more numeric content as well as a wider range of characters eg $, %, ★ signs

Third Level

Candidates must be able to:

2.1   Change orientation from portrait to landscape

2.2   Print a landscape document

12.1   Print multiple copies of a document

12.2   Print parts of a document: blocks or pre-defined pages

14.1   Use standard correction signs as defined in Appendix A

14.2   Use non-standard but straightforward manuscript correction signs

Timing yourself

Each assignment at each level is given a time allowance. You must complete your assignment within the stated time. Your tutor will tell you when to start and when to finish work. You have 30 minutes to complete each **First Level** assignment. **Second Level** and **Third Level** assignments will have a time allowance of between 30 minutes and 60 minutes each. The time allowed is stated clearly at the front of the assignment pack.

The time allocation is related directly to the amount of work that must be done for successful completion of the assignment. This includes preparation time and checking time. You may print after the time has elapsed, but you may not make any further changes to your document.

It is a good idea to read through the assignment carefully before you start work. Read the instructions at the top of the page carefully. You must follow them all. Additional instructions will be given as you proceed through the assignment. It is important that you follow them correctly.

Always leave time to check your work carefully. Many candidates fail simply because they have not identified simple errors for themselves.

Creating, saving and retrieving files

Some documents will have been put on your computer system in advance of the examination. A Tutor pack accompanies the assignments, and your tutor will have keyed in the appropriate documents and saved them under a file name that will be given to you. You must then retrieve these files and make the amendments that are shown on the candidate's copy of the assignment.

Other assignments, however, require that you create a new document and save your work under an appropriate file name. No file name will be given to you. It does not matter what you call your document, but you should make a note of its name because you must be able to retrieve it again if necessary.

It is a good idea to save your work regularly while you are working on each assignment. A print-out of each assignment must be produced for marking. No credit can be given for work that has been lost.

Entering text

Assignments at all three levels require that you can enter text accurately. The assignments at **First Level** require basic keyboarding skills, and much of the text to be entered is from typed copy. The vocabulary is simple, and specialised words will not be used. You will always be asked to include your name at the bottom of the document.

An example of Assignment 1 at First Level is given on page 7.

EXERCISE 1.1

ASSIGNMENT 1 – Candidate's Copy

1 Key in the following text.

2 Add your name at the bottom left.

3 Proofread your work and print out a copy on A4 paper with a justified right-hand margin.

AIR TRAVEL

In the 1950s, air travel was a luxury which only the rich could afford. The average person would travel by train or by boat. Overseas travel was time-consuming and uncomfortable, and the traveller would arrive at his destination tired and dirty.

Nowadays most people travel by air. It is the fastest and easiest way to travel long distances. Most large cities have an airport within easy reach. Each year it becomes easier to buy a ticket, board an aeroplane and arrive at a faraway destination within hours of leaving home.

For long distances, it is often cheaper to travel by air.

Try it for yourself! Copy the words exactly, but do not follow the line endings. It does not matter if your text is in a different font. Check your work carefully before printing. A correct version appears on page 158.

At **Second** and **Third Levels**, there will be fewer exercises requiring straight copy typing. The vocabulary used will be more specialised and a large amount of the text will be handwritten. However, the task will be straightforward and unambiguous. Foreign words will never be used in English assignments.

Making amendments and additions

Some assignments ask you to change the text that has already been saved for you by your tutor. Handwritten words will be added to the document. You must insert them at the appropriate position in the text. At **First Level**, the words will be written clearly and in full. Sometimes the words will appear in a balloon with an arrow to indicate their exact location in the text. Follow the instructions carefully.

An example of an assignment at **First Level** that requires text amendments and additions is given on page 8.

EXERCISE 1.2

FREEDOM HOLIDAYS
45-49 Charles Street
LEICESTER LE1 4JK

Mrs S Robertson
2 The Square
LUTTERWORTH
LE9 2DF

Dear ~~Madam~~ Mrs Robertson

Thank you for your letter requesting details of coach holidays to [Spain and] Portugal. I enclose a selection of brochures, which I hope you will find useful.

I should like to draw your attention to two holidays that are [exceptionally] good value. The first is a fly-drive holiday. A scheduled flight to Lisbon is followed by an 8-day coach tour around Portugal, with holiday-makers staying in traditional coaching inns.

A detailed itinerary is included in the brochure. The all-inclusive price of £650 makes this holiday a real bargain.

The second is a 10-day coach tour around Southern Spain, with scheduled flights to and from Malaga. At only £750 per person, this is also excellent value for money.

Please let me know if you would like me to check availability on these holidays. I will need to know departure dates [and the number of people travelling]

I look forward to hearing from you soon.

Yours ~~faithfully~~ sincerely

Tina George
Office Manager

Encs

Try it for yourself! The answer appears on page 159.

At **Second** and **Third Levels**, you will be asked to make more complicated amendments to the text. However, the handwriting used will always be legible and the exact location for the inserted text clearly marked.

Working from manuscript

As mentioned above, amendments to text at **First Level** will be indicated in handwriting. They will be accompanied by the appropriate correction sign. The correction sign will appear in the left or right margin. At **Second** and **Third Levels**, much of the text will be handwritten, and correction signs will be used to indicate how the text should be changed.

Figure 1.1 is a list of correction signs that will be used throughout the assignments at all levels.

Sign in Margin	Meaning	Instruction	Example
lc	lower case	change capital letter(s) into small letter(s)	The cat Sat on the mat
uc or caps	upper case	change small letter(s) into capital letter(s)	United states of America
NP	new paragraph	divide continuous text at point indicated by // or [	... end of the working day. [It was apparent that ...
run on	run on	join the two paragraphs together as shown	... working during college hours. Staff will be offered ...
trs	transpose	change the order of two items, vertically or horizontally	pepper and salt Britain Brazil
ꝺ	delete	leave out the word(s) crossed through	many people were ~~very~~ worried about ...
ʎ	insert	include the word(s) indicated	I was absolutely delighted to ....
close up	close up	reduce the amount of space between words	... the message took a long time ...
stet	stet (let it stand)	leave in place the word(s) originally crossed through	He was very anxious ~~worried~~

Figure 1.1 Correction signs

Where correction signs are used, there will be a mark in the text and an instruction in the margin on the same line.

An extract from a **Second Level** assignment that includes correction signs is given on page 10.

EXERCISE 1.3

> ⌐ booking
> Thank you for choosing Comlon Contacts as your preferred⎮agency.
> We offer a wide range of facilities, which range from restaurant and
> hotel bookings to large-scale corporate entertainment. We look
> forward to forging a long and ~~lasting~~ business relationship with you.
>   *successful*
> NP [Here are a few ideas for you to consider. *Do you regularly*
> *of*   *take clients ~~out~~ to lunch at top-class restaurants?*
> *We can arrange attractive discounts for you.⎫*
> *run on* ⌐————————————————————————————
> *trs* *Consult our comprehensive list of <u>restaurants</u>⎮participating*
> *to see whether your favourite appears. When*
> *entertaining clients, we can also obtain tickets for*
> *uc* *all the leading west end shows at a fraction of*
> *the advertised price.*
>   *6521*
> *Want to know more? Give us a call on 0171 438 ~~6531~~ now!*

Try it for yourself! The answer appears on page 160.

Using abbreviations

At **First Level**, all words in the assignments will be written in full. At
Second and **Third Levels**, however, selected words may be abbreviated,
and you must expand them whenever they occur. There will be no
punctuation following the abbreviation. You must identify the abbreviation
and expand it in full each time it occurs.

Days of the week and months of the year will often be abbreviated. You
must always type them in full. Similarly, words such as 'Street', 'Road' and
'Avenue' may appear in abbreviated form (St, Rd, Ave). Again, they
should always be expanded. However, abbreviations such as 'etc', 'ie' and
'eg' should not be expanded. The ampersand (&) which appears in company
names should not be changed to 'and', but in all other cases 'and' should
be typed in full.

A full list of abbreviations appears below. Check them carefully to make
sure that you understand their meaning and can spell the expanded
words correctly.

Abbreviations used at Second and Third Levels

Abbreviation	Word in full	Abbreviation	Word in full
approx	approximately	org	organisation
asap	as soon as possible	poss	possible
cat	catalogue	ref	reference
co(s)	company/ies	shd	should
dept	department	temp	temporary
dr	dear	th	that
immed	immediately	tho	though
info	information	wd	would
no	number	yr	year/your
Mon	Monday	Jan	January
Tue	Tuesday	Feb	February
Wed	Wednesday	Mar	March
Thur	Thursday	Apr	April
Fri	Friday	May	May
Sat	Saturday	Jun	June
Sun	Sunday	Jul	July
		Aug	August
		Sept	September
		Oct	October
		Nov	November
		Dec	December
Ave	Avenue	Pl	Place
Cres	Crescent	Rd	Road
Dr	Drive	Sq	Square
Pk	Park	St	Street
Yrs ffly	Yours faithfully	Yrs sncly	Yours sincerely

Try Exercise 1.4 (see page 12) on abbreviations. The answer appears on page 160.

EXERCISE 1.4

> This org is justly proud of its fine reputation. We employ approx 300 members of staff within our co and this no increases during the summer months when we take on additional temp staff.
>
> If you wd like to receive further info and an application form, please contact us immed on extension 265. We shall be interviewing early in Apr and shd be pleased to hear from you.

Following instructions

It is important that you follow every instruction that appears on each assignment. At **First Level**, most instructions will appear in a numbered list above the assignment. These instructions will tell you to create or retrieve a document, make a series of amendments to it, put your name on it, proofread it carefully and print out a copy.

Figure 1.2 is an example of a set of instructions at **First Level**.

ASSIGNMENT 3 – Candidate's Copy

1 Key in the following information and retain the line spacing.

2 Centre each line and embolden where indicated.

3 Add your name at the bottom left.

4 Proofread, store on disk and print a copy on A4 paper.

Figure 1.2   First Level instructions

At **Second Level**, most instructions will be in the numbered list above the assignment. However, other instructions will be given as you proceed through the task. Some will be in balloons. Others will appear alongside the text to be amended. Arrows may be used to direct you to the text to be altered.

Figure 1.3 (see page 13) is an example of a set of instructions at **Second Level**.

ASSIGNMENT 1 – Candidate's Copy

1 Recall the following document to your screen, saved under [file name], and edit as shown.

2 Repaginate sensibly and number each page at the bottom.

3 Leave 25 mm (1 inch) between each section.

4 Centre each section heading.

5 Change both margins to 38 mm (1.5 inches) and use a fully justified right margin.

6 Insert a header CONFERENCES at the top right of the page.

7 Change meeting to seminar wherever it occurs within the text.

Figure 1.3   Second Level instructions

As you can see, although the changes to be made are more numerous and more complicated at **Second Level** than at **First Level**, they are still clearly explained and easy to follow.

At **Third Level**, there are fewer instructions at the top of the page. At this level, it is expected that you will repeatedly apply an instruction given once to ensure consistency.

All instructions at all levels will be given in clear, simple English.

Displaying your work attractively

All work produced should be displayed as attractively as possible. You should aim to incorporate new text within a document and still maintain the overall appearance of the document.

All assignments at all three levels will be produced using fully blocked style and open punctuation. This means that all lines start at the left margin and no punctuation is used in dates, addresses, salutations or complimentary closes. Punctuation is used normally in continuous text, however.

There is no prescribed way to lay out a letter. However, the layout given in Figure 1.4 (see page 14) is the one favoured by most candidates, and, if you are unsure of where to position an item of information, this would be a good layout to follow.

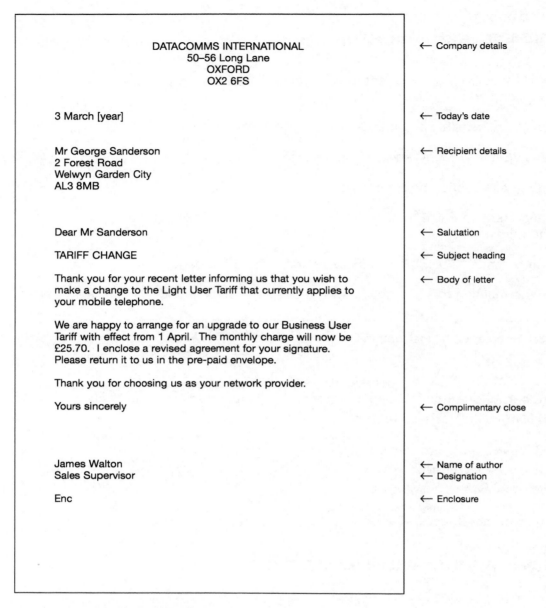

Figure 1.4   Favoured letter layout

In **First Level** assignments, you will be asked to insert the date on a letter or on a memorandum. A date is not needed on other documents.

Specific instructions may be given at **Second** and **Third Levels** to include the date on other documents as required.

Proofreading

It is absolutely essential that you check your work very carefully. **First Level** assignments are quite short and are relatively easy to check, but longer assignments at **Second** and **Third Levels** can be more difficult.

Take care when you key in your text. Try to make as few typographical errors as possible. When you have finished the assignment, check your work on screen. Use a document holder so that your original assignment is level with your screen. Check your work word by word.

Spellcheck facilities are useful, but they will not find words that are correctly spelled but incorrectly used. If an alternative spelling is suggested, you must decide whether to follow the version shown in the assignment or accept the alternative. Whichever you choose, you must be consistent. You will not be penalised for alternative spellings.

Printing

When you have completed your assignment, you must produce a print-out for marking. At **First Level**, all assignments will fit easily on to one page. Only one copy of each document is required, and the paper orientation will be portrait (narrow edge at the top). The instruction about printing will always appear at the top of the assignment.

At **Second Level**, some assignments fit on to one page, but Assignments 1 and 3 are multi-page documents consisting of three pages of text. However, only one copy of each is required, and the paper orientation is portrait. Again, the instruction about printing will appear at the top of the assignment.

Multiple copies are required only in **Third Level** assignments. Clear instructions will be given when more than one copy of a document is required. At **Third Level**, you must also be able to print out selected portions of a document. This could be just one page or a section of a page. You will also be asked to print out in landscape format (wide edge at the top). Printing instructions at **Third Level** may appear anywhere within the document.

HELPFUL HINTS

- **Read through the assignment before starting work.**
- **Save your work regularly under a meaningful file name.**
- **Learn to recognise manuscript correction signs.**
- **Learn the list of abbreviations.**
- **Make sure that you follow every instruction.**
- **Use open punctuation and blocked style for simplicity.**
- **Proofread your work carefully for errors.**
- **Print out a final copy on A4 portrait (unless otherwise instructed).**

2

Text enhancement

After carefully studying this chapter, you should be able to:

1 *follow specific instructions to centre, embolden and underline text;*

2 *understand what the expression 'justified right margin' means;*

3 *use appropriate bullets or special characters within a document;*

4 *make changes to the font size;*

5 *use borders and shading as instructed.*

Extended Syllabus references

First Level

Candidates must be able to:

  5.1 Use the following text enhancement features when entering or editing text:

    5.1.1 embolden

    5.1.2 underline

  6.1 Use the following formatting facilities when entering or editing text:

    6.1.1 justified/ragged right–hand margins

    6.1.2 centring text

    6.1.3 simple tabs

Third Level

Candidates must be able to:

  3.1 Select appropriate font styles from Courier, Times New Roman and 3 others as provided by Centre

  3.2 Select appropriate font sizes as identified by point size

  3.3 Select and use italic font where appropriate

  3.4 Include special characters (symbols) within text, eg fractions, accents

  5.1 Create a border around text

  5.2 Create a box and lines within a table

  5.3 Shade a box

Using centre, bold and underline

At **First Level** you will be given specific instructions when to use the centre, bold or underline functions. The instructions will normally be handwritten next to the text which should be amended. A complete section of text may have to be centred and emboldened, or the instruction may refer only to individual words. In all cases, you will know exactly how much text to change.

Figure 2.1 is an example of an assignment at **First Level**.

---

1   Key in the following text exactly as copy.

2   Centre each line and embolden and underline where indicated.

3   Add your name at the bottom left.

4   Proofread, store on disk and print a copy on A4 paper.

CRAVEN PARK SPORTS CENTRE
DAWLISH   } *bold*
SOUTH DEVON

SIMPLE RULES FOR A HEALTHY LIFESTYLE   — *bold and underline*

Eat three meals a day - with the emphasis on breakfast
(reduce saturated fat and meat)

Take a moderate amount of exercise!

Get a minimum of seven hours sleep a night

DO NOT SMOKE   — *bold*

Drink at least 2 litres of fresh water each day

Do not eat between meals

Keep your weight around the average for your height and build

Avoid unnecessary stressful situations

BE HEALTHY AND BE HAPPY   — *bold and underline*

Figure 2.1   A First Level assignment

Try it for yourself! The answer appears on page 161.

At **Second** and **Third Levels**, you will also be asked to make specific amendments to the text. The instructions may appear within the assignment itself (as above) or you may be given an instruction at the beginning of the assignment. If an instruction is given at the beginning, you are expected to apply the amendment consistently throughout the assignment.

Sometimes you will be asked to display your work attractively. This instruction means that you can use any form of enhancement (centre, bold, underline, italics, etc) to make your work look as attractive as possible.

A **Second Level** assignment asking you to display your work attractively is given below.

EXERCISE 2.2

The following document has been left for you to produce. Use your own judgement with regard to display and print out a copy.

SPECIAL OFFER!

DISCOVER MADRID

For only £350 per person

Fly away to Spain this summer and visit one
of Europe's most attractive/cities. [For only   *capital*   NP
£350 per person you can enjoy

        of   scheduled flights from your regional airport
3 nights' ~~full board~~ accommodation in a
4-star hotel
free buffet breakfast each day
trs   free transfers from/and/to the airport in Madrid
free use of swimming pool and health club
free half-day coach tour of main tourist sights

To make your reservation or to obtain ~~further~~ *further*
details of this fantastic offer, contact us on

0800 453 6921

Don't miss the chance to discover Spain's majestic
capital!

HAPPY HOLIDAYS!

Try it for yourself! An answer appears on page 162 but your version might not be the same. This does not matter. The important thing is that the text is accurate and your work is attractively presented.

Using justified margins

Within the LCCIEB Practical Word Processing assignments, the instruction 'Use a justified right-hand margin' means that *both* margins must be justified (ie not ragged). Some candidates produce work which has a justified right margin but a ragged left margin. You will never be asked to do this.

At **First Level**, Assignment 1 always requires a justified right-hand margin. The text is keyed in by the candidate, so you can choose when to justify the text, either before you begin to type or when you have completed the document.

At **Second** and **Third Levels**, text which has been keyed in by the tutor in advance of the examination date may have to be amended.

Where no instruction is given, you may decide for yourself which style of right-hand margin you prefer.

Using bullets and special characters

Bullets are not usually required at **First** and **Second Levels**. There will be no specific instruction to use them but if you are asked to display your work attractively and the text lends itself to the use of bullets, then you may use them if you wish.

Third Level assignments will incorporate bullets and/or special characters in the text. You may use any design of bullet you wish, but it is advisable to use a design and size that is appropriate to the work being displayed. Special characters may include the use of fractions, accents and other commonly used symbols (eg °, (c) and ÷).

An extract from a **Third Level** assignment that requires the use of bullets is given on page 20.

EXERCISE 2.3

> FIVE GOOD REASONS WHY <u>YOU</u> SHOULD CHOOSE A COMLON CREDIT CARD ...
>
> ✓   low APR of just 6.5% plus no annual fee
> ✓   up to 56 days' interest-free credit if you pay your balance off in full each month
> ✓   choice of Visa or Mastercard
> ✓   accepted by 15 million outlets worldwide
> ✓   optional card protection cover
>
> PLUS a £200 discount when you transfer the balance from your current card!
>
> CAN YOU AFFORD TO TURN DOWN THIS FANTASTIC OFFER?
>
> For further details, telephone us on 0800 962 534 now. We look forward to receiving your call.

Try it for yourself! The answer appears on page 163.

Changing font sizes and styles

There is also no requirement in the **First** and **Second Level** syllabus to make changes to font sizes and styles.

At **Third Level**, however, specific instructions will be given to change the font to a given point size. However, a specific font style will not be requested. Examiners cannot be certain that all candidates have access to the same font styles and so you may make your own choice of font style.

In certain situations at **Third Level**, it may be necessary for you to reduce the font size to ensure that the document fits on to one page.

An extract from a **Third Level** assignment that requires a specific change to the font size is given on page 21.

EXERCISE 2.4

Try it for yourself! A suggested answer appears on page 163.

Using borders and shading

Borders and shading are another feature which only appear in **Third Level** assignments. At **First** and **Second Levels**, you will not be asked to use borders and shading at all. In fact, if you do put a border around a table at **Second Level**, you will incur an error for doing so.

At **Third Level**, borders and shading will be requested for specific sections of text and also within the complex table. The choice of border and depth of shading will be left to the candidate. However, the shading should be light enough to allow the text to be clearly legible.

Exercise 2.5 is a short extract from a **Third Level** assignment. Use this exercise to practise borders and shading around a main heading.

EXERCISE 2.5

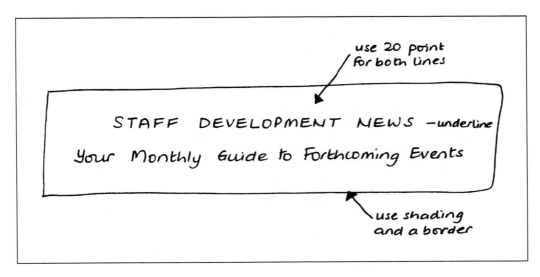

A suggested answer appears on page 164 but yours may look quite different in terms of the border chosen and the depth of the shading. However, as long as your border surrounds the text as requested, your work is perfectly acceptable.

HELPFUL HINTS

- Make sure that you have followed instructions to centre, embolden or underline text wherever the instructions appear.

- Be consistent in your approach if the instruction appears only once.

- Do not change the appearance of text unless you are told to do so.

- Remember that a justified right margin means that *both* margins should be justified.

- Only use bullets which are appropriate for the document.

- You may make your own choice of font style.

- Use borders and shading only when instructed – do not add borders to text or tables which do not need them.

3

Formatting features

After carefully studying this chapter, you should be able to:

1 *follow specific instructions to change line spacing;*

2 *follow specific instructions to change right and left margins;*

3 *follow specific instructions to indent text;*

4 *leave space of a specified size;*

5 *move blocks of text;*

6 *rearrange the order of text.*

Extended Syllabus references

Second Level

Candidates must be able to:

1.1 Set specified margins

1.2 Change pre-set margins

1.3 Set different margins within the document

1.4 Indent sections

1.5 Set line spacing

1.6 Change pre-set line spacing

1.7 Set different line spacing within the document

5.1 Define a block of text

5.2 Move a block of text

5.3 Delete a block of text

5.4 Copy a block of text

9.1 Rearrange a list of items in alphabetical order

9.2 Rearrange a list of items in numerical order

9.3 Rearrange columns in alphabetical order

9.4 Rearrange columns in numerical order

(continued)

Extended Syllabus references (continued)

9.5 Insert text at a marked location eg marked with an alphabet character or an asterisk

9.6 Rearrange text in marked order eg marked with an alphabet character or a number

13.1 Leave specified space between paragraphs

13.2 Leave specified space at right or left of blocks of text

Note: Space to be specified in both inches and centimetres

Third Level

Candidates must be able to:

8.1 Centre documents vertically and horizontally

8.2 Indent paragraphs from both margins to a specified size

9.1 Reorganise information logically, ie paragraph order

9.2 Reorganise information selectively, ie only marked information

Changing line spacing

Although line spacing changes do not appear at **First Level**, there is one assignment where you may be required to leave at least one clear line between items. This is Assignment 3, in which you must key in a document which does not use single line spacing throughout. As the lines will usually be short, it is quite acceptable to press the enter key more than once at the end of each line in order to leave the required space. You do not have to format the line spacing in any other way if you do not wish to do so.

Exercise 3.1 (see page 25) is a sample Assignment 3 at **First Level** that you can use to practise changing line spacing.

EXERCISE 3.1

1   Key in the following text and retain the line spacing.

2   Centre each line and embolden where indicated.

3   Keep the line endings as shown.

4   Add your name at the bottom left.

5   Proofread, store on disk and print a copy on A4 paper.

TRAVELLERS' WORLD   — *bold and underline*

✱

We are pleased to announce the opening of our new

TRAVEL CLINIC   — *bold*

at

52 Sloane Street   } *bold*
LONDON EC4 2JR

Telephone: 0171 349 8651   — *underline*

We have a full range of vaccines in stock and give
practical advice on the prevention of tropical diseases

Mosquito nets, insect repellants and water-purifying kits
are also available at low cost

For FREE advice   *bold*

call in and meet our professional staff
who will be delighted to help you

✱

No appointment necessary   — *underline*

✱ Leave 3 clear line spaces at these points

Try it for yourself! The answer appears on page 164.

At **Second** and **Third Levels**, however, your line spacing changes will affect continuous text, so it is important that you format your work correctly. Most assignments require only certain paragraphs to be changed. In many cases, the majority of the document will appear in single line spacing, with specific sections appearing in double line spacing. A change from single to double, or from double to single, is the only change that will be required. Try to leave equal space above and below the affected paragraph.

Exercise 3.2 (see page 26) is an extract from a **Second Level** assignment that requires a line spacing change.

EXERCISE 3.2

COMLON DIRECT

INSURANCE WITH A DIFFERENCE!

} *bold*

constantly

At Comlon Direct, we/aim to improve the services we offer to our customers. We seek to offer you competitive rates with guaranteed monthly repayments so that you can plan ahead with confidence.

That's why we are pleased to announce our new personal loan for existing customers only. With an APR of only 11.5% this makes a Comlon Direct personal loan the cheapest on the market. *So, if you're thinking of buying a new car, making those long-awaited home improvements or treating the family to an exotic holiday, this could be the opportunity that you've been waiting for!*

double line spacing for this paragraph

Take a look at the enclosed table to see just how small your monthly repayments will be. Choose your own repayment period to suit your personal needs. Then simply complete the application form on page 4 and return it to Comlon Direct. We look forward to hearing from you soon.

Changing margins

At **First Level**, you will not be asked to make any changes to margins, except to justify the right hand margin (see Chapter 2).

Second and **Third Level** assignments, however, include instructions to change margins for an entire document or for a specific section of text. Whenever a margin change is given, the width of the margin is expressed in centimetres or millimetres with the imperial measurement in brackets immediately afterwards, eg 7.5 cm (3 inches). If the word inches is not used, inch marks will be used, eg 38 mm (1.5″).

If the margin change applies to the entire document, the instruction will be given at the beginning of the assignment, see Figure 3.1 on page 27.

ASSIGNMENT 1

1 Recall the following document to your screen, saved under [file name] and edit as shown.

2 Repaginate sensibly and number each page at the bottom.

3 Change the left margin to 5 cm (2 inches) and the right margin to 3.8 cm (1.5 inches). Use a justified right margin.

Figure 3.1   Example of instructions asking for a margin change

If, however, the margin change applies to only one section of the text, the instruction will appear as a handwritten, marginal instruction.

Changes to top and bottom margins may also be required at **Third Level**. Such changes would normally include a shortening of the page length by increasing the size of the top or bottom margins or both. As with the right and left margins, measurements will be given in centimetres or millimetres and in inches.

At **Third Level** you may also be asked to centre text vertically on the page. This can be done manually, automatically or by changing the top and bottom margins.

Indenting portions of text

At **Second Level**, you will be asked only to indent a portion of text from the left margin. Once again, the instruction will be handwritten and will appear in the margin next to the text which will be affected by the change. The size of the indent will be expressed in centimetres or millimetres and in inches. It will never be expressed in character spaces.

At **Third Level**, you will be required to indent a portion of text from both margins. Clear instructions will be given as to the size of the indent required.

Exercise 3.3 (see page 28) is an extract from an assignment which gives a marginal instruction to change the left margin for a section of text.

EXERCISE 3.3

THREE STAR CONTRACT

Our Three S— C— provides repair cover for all your gas systems and appliances and a yearly safety check which finds and repairs any faults.)

run on

We provide this service to our customers for home systems only. Check your details carefully on the enclosed agreement.

indent this section 38 mm (1.5 inches) from the left margin

The price of your Three Star Contract is printed on the agreement form. You can pay by direct debit once a year or once a month, by debit or credit *trs* card or by a single payment each year for the year ahead. Whichever method of payment you ~~decide to~~ choose, we will end the agreement if you miss any payment that is due.

Check the agreement now, add your signature and return it to us in the enclosed pre-paid envelope.

Try it for yourself! The answer appears on page 165.

Leaving space of a specified size

At **Second** and **Third Levels**, you are asked to leave specified amounts of space between paragraphs. This amount may be expressed in centimetres or millimetres and in inches or it may be expressed in clear line spaces. The instruction is usually preceded by the words 'at least', and, if so, the space does not have to be exact, although you should be consistent in the amount of space you leave between similar items.

Second and **Third Level** assignments also include instructions to leave a space for a photograph or a logo. Measurements will be given in centimetres or millimetres and in inches, and the horizontal and vertical measurements may not be identical. The instruction will be contained in a hand–drawn box of approximately the size required and will be handwritten. The instruction will always include the words 'at least'.

No penalty will be incurred if the space you leave is larger than that specified. However, if the space is smaller than the measurement given, you will be penalised.

The space should *not* be surrounded by a box.

Exercise 3.4 is an extract from a **Second Level** assignment that requires space to be left for two photographs.

EXERCISE 3.4

OUR TEACHING STAFF

USE A JUSTIFIED
RIGHT MARGIN

leave a space at least
64 mm (2.5 inches) wide
by 38 mm (1.5 inches)
deep for a photograph

All our teachers are native speakers.
They hold professional teaching
qualifications and have had many
years of teaching experience in the
United Kingdom and overseas.
Several have specialised in the study of
linguistics
and all are experts in the use of new
technology to support language
learning.

OUR COURSES

All our courses are designed to help you master the English
language. You will have plenty of opportunity to listen,
speak, read and write in your lessons. With only 12 students
in each class, you can be sure of support and help from
your teacher.

OUR CAMPUS

Located close to the main shopping
streets of Central London, our campus
is attractive and modern and our
classrooms provide a pleasant
learning environment. Three
language laboratories support
individual learning programmes and
an open-access computer centre
ensures that you have the opportunity
to use modern software packages.

leave a space at least
64 mm (2.5 inches) wide
by 38 mm (1.5 inches)
deep for a photograph

For further details of this year's courses and an application
form, please contact Robert Goodman on 0800 345 871.

Try it for yourself! The correct version appears on page 166.

Moving blocks of text

At **First Level**, movement of text is limited to the transposition of words and to joining and separating paragraphs.

At **Second** and **Third Levels**, however, text movement becomes more complicated and may involve the movement of sentences, paragraphs or columns of text.

Sometimes the new location is indicated by an arrow which directs you to the exact position required. Alternatively, the text to be moved may be encircled and a handwritten instruction given to 'insert at B'. A letter B will appear at a new position in the text.

Exercise 3.5 is an extract from a **Second Level** assignment. Try it to see how it works.

EXERCISE 3.5

WELCOME TO COMTECH INTERNATIONAL! — bold and centre

(A)

OUR CAMPUS

area just

Our campus is located in a quiet residential ~~suburb~~ a short distance from Regent's Park. It comprises three attractive, modern buildings which house the teaching accommodation and the administration centre. A self-service restaurant and barbecue area overlook landscaped gardens. The local shopping area offers a wide *range* ~~variety~~ of amenities including bookshops, banks and a post office.

OUR COURSES

We offer ~~as~~ a wide range of courses, ranging from a ~~brief~~ *half-day* introduction to computing to a programming course ~~which lasts~~ *lasting* for two weeks. You will find a full listing of our courses in our prospectus. However, if you require a course tailored to your own ~~personal~~ requirements, contact our Course Administrator and we can arrange an individualised course just for you.

OUR TEACHING STAFF

Our team of teaching staff consists of highly qualified specialists who are not only experts in the latest software, but who also have attained professional teaching qualifications. Whatever ~~course~~ you come to learn, you will be in very safe hands!

trs

Come and join us soon!
We look forward to hearing from you.
COMTECH INTERNATIONAL — TRAINING AT ITS BEST!

bold and centre

INSERT AT (A) ABOVE

Each year millions of people undertake training to perfect their skills in the latest computer software packages. We at Comtech International pride ourselves on delivering courses of the highest standard to more than 20,000 students each year. Come and join us ....

Try it for yourself! Check your work against the correct version on page 167.

At **Third Level**, you may be asked to rearrange the order of paragraphs or headings. This might involve arranging paragraphs into numerical or alphabetical order. Clear instructions will always be given, either at the top of the assignment or at the position in the document where the amendment is to take place.

HELPFUL HINTS

- Make your line spacing and margin changes *after* you have keyed in all the text of your document.

- Try to leave equal space above and below the text which has had its line spacing changed.

- Be exact when indenting portions of text from the left and right margins.

- Space left for a photograph will be approximate – make sure that you have left *at least* the specified amount of space.

- When moving blocks of text, be careful to reposition the text in the exact new location.

- When rearranging the order of paragraphs, be sure to check that you have included all the necessary text.

4

Multi-page documents

After carefully studying this chapter, you should be able to:

1 *appreciate the need to use sensible page breaks;*

2 *follow instructions relating to the numbering of pages;*

3 *use headers and footers;*

4 *understand the procedures involved in the search-and-replace function.*

Extended Syllabus references

Second Level

Candidates must be able to:

2.1 Search and replace globally

2.2 Search and replace selectively

2.3 Check case match

3.1 Insert a header at left, centre or right of margin

3.2 Insert a footer at left, centre or right of margin

4.1 Paginate document starting with page 1

4.2 Repaginate document to include sensible page breaks

4.3 Insert a manual page break

4.4 Delete a manual page break

Third Level

Candidates must be able to:

7.1 Number pages, except for first page

7.2 Number pages from a specified number

Using sensible page breaks

There are no multi-page documents at **First Level**. Each assignment is designed to fit on one page. Therefore you do not need to know how to number pages or insert headers and footers.

At **Second** and **Third Levels**, at least two assignments at each level will incorporate several pages. You are instructed or expected to use sensible page breaks within these documents. This means that you must not split a paragraph so that one half appears at the bottom of the first page and the remainder appears at the top of the next. Where possible, you must end your page at the end of one paragraph and before the next one begins. Sometimes this will mean that you will have to delete a page break which has been inserted by your tutor in the tutor copy. You may do so if this means that your work fits on the page better. Your final print-out may not look like the marking copy, but you will not be penalised if you have used sensible page breaks.

It is a good idea to check what your finished document will look like by using the print preview option within your word-processing software. In this way you can make final adjustments prior to printing out your work.

Numbering pages

At **Second** and **Third Levels**, it is expected that documents of more than one page will bear page numbers. Unless otherwise specified, all pages should be numbered (including the first page). Sometimes the position of the page number will be given (top right, bottom centre) and you should follow such an instruction carefully. If no instruction is given about the position, you may make your own decision as to position. When they are given a choice, most candidates choose the bottom centre as their preferred page number position.

At **Second Level**, multi-page documents will have page 1 numbered 1. Subsequent pages will be numbered 2 and 3.

At **Third Level**, you may be asked to number pages when the first page is, for example, 6. You may also be asked to omit the page number from the first page of a multi-page document.

Using headers and footers

At **Second Level**, you will be asked to insert a header or a footer or both on a multi-page document. The position of the header and footer will always be given, ie at the left, centre or right of the page. You must also follow the copy regarding the use of capitals and emboldening. The header and footer must appear on all pages. Be sure to check that this will happen before printing out your work.

At **Third Level**, the instructions are more demanding. You may be asked to include a header on all pages, but to suppress the footer on the first page. Practise until you can do this quickly and accurately.

Figure 4.1 contains some instructions from a **Third Level** assignment relating to headers and footers.

ASSIGNMENT 5 – Candidate's Copy

1 Key in the following document, expanding abbreviations.

2 Use a justified right margin.

3 Number the second page only at the bottom right.

4 Use a header SUMMER COURSES on each page. Embolden the text and position the header at the top right.

5 Proofread carefully.

6 Save your work and print out a copy on A4 portrait.

Figure 4.1   Third Level instructions about headers and footers

If you are unsure how to do any part of this assignment, practise on a blank document until you can confidently perform the task. You will be able to practise further in an exercise in Chapter 5.

Using search and replace

The search-and-replace function is tested in Assignment 1 at **Second Level**. This assignment is partially pre-keyed by your tutor, and you are asked to replace a given word or phrase with another whenever it occurs within the document. The instruction to make the change will appear at the top of the assignment.

Search and replace can be done manually or automatically. However you do it, it is very important that you check your work very carefully and make sure that *only* the requested words have been changed. Each failure to make the change will incur a penalty. There are usually between 3 and 5 changes to be made. It is a good idea to make search and replace the last function you perform before final proofreading and printing.

Exercise 4.1 tests the use of search and replace.

EXERCISE 4.1

---

1   Key in the text below, making amendments as shown.
2   Use double line spacing and a justified right hand margin.
3   Change brochure to catalogue wherever it occurs within the text.
4   Proofread your work carefully and print out a copy.

Pricing Policy — capitals

                                          ruling
The prices quoted in this brochure are those in place at the time of printing. Due to

circumstances beyond our control, prices may have to be altered up or down,
                                      purchase   appear
including any alterations to the rate of tax. The correct price will be shown on your

despatch note. If an item is not acceptable, it may be returned, providing it is sent

back within 14 days and is in perfect condition

All prices shown in this brochure are cash prices. There is a service charge on

extended credit accounts. Please contact your local agent for further details of

¶ current rates.

Homecare plc reserves the right to amend credit charges,
to withdraw credit or, with prior written notice, to close
an account.

Try it for yourself! Check your answer on page 168. Did you check that the search–and–replace function made all the necessary changes?

HELPFUL HINTS

- Use sensible page breaks so that single lines of text are not left at the bottom or top of the page.

- Use your print preview option to see what your document looks like prior to printing.

- Follow the instructions carefully with regard to the page-numbering position.

- Number the pages of all multi-page documents.

- Include header and footer information on all pages unless otherwise instructed.

- Always check that headers and footers appear on your document before printing.

- Check that the search-and-replace function has made the required changes accurately.

5

Tabulation

After carefully studying this chapter, you should be able to:

1 *identify the need to set simple tabs for effective display;*

2 *arrange work in columns without borders or gridlines;*

3 *use more advanced functions to produce a complex table incorporating borders, gridlines and shading;*

4 *use multi-level numbering to display text.*

Extended Syllabus references

First Level

    6.1 Use the following formatting facilities when entering or editing text:

        6.1.1 justified/ragged right-hand margins

        6.1.2 centring text

        6.1.3 simple tabs

Second Level

Candidates must be able to:

  8.1 Create a simple table up to 4 columns

  8.2 Input text and numeric information

  8.3 Print table, unruled, and without border

Third Level

Candidates must be able to:

  2.1 Change orientation from portrait to landscape

  2.2 Print a landscape document

  4.1 Create a table with complex merged and split cells

  4.2 Include lines within and around table, using boxes, borders and shading

  6.1 Use numbering facilities to number paragraphs

  6.2 Indent numbered paragraphs from left margin

Setting simple tabs

At **First Level**, you will not be required to key in a table, but you may be asked to number paragraph headings or produce a list which is indented from the left margin. To enable you to do this, it may be necessary to set a simple tab so that the number appears at the left margin and the text is indented evenly from the left margin.

Exercise 5.1 is part of an assignment at **First Level** requiring the use of simple tabs.

EXERCISE 5.1

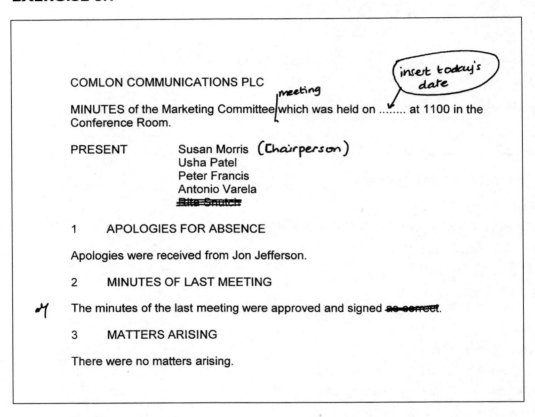

Try it for yourself! The correct version appears on page 169.

Arranging work in columns

At **Second Level**, you will be asked to produce a simple table, of up to 4 columns, incorporating text and numbers. To do this successfully, you will have to set tabs or use the tables function within your word-processing software. You must not include printed gridlines or a border in your table. Equal spacing between columns is not required. You must ensure, however, that each item within a column starts at the same point. You may also be asked to reorganise the text into alphabetical or numerical order. This can be done before or after keying in the text.

Exercise 5.2 is a **Second Level** assignment on display in columns.

EXERCISE 5.2

Please rearrange Course Titles into alphabetical order

SHORT COURSE PROGRAMME — bold and underline

CAREER AND PERSONAL DEVELOPMENT — bold

The following courses will be held over the next three months. I shall be forwarding further details and exact dates to Section Leaders shortly. If you are interested in any of these courses, please contact Gita on Extension 246.

column headings in bold with underline

Course Title	Location	Duration
Time Management	Head Office	1 day
Team Building Techniques	Coventry	2 days
Assertiveness Training	Bristol	1 day
Surviving Stress	Head Office	1 day
Presentation Skills	Head Office	2 days
Using the Internet	Coventry	1 day

Please remember that a minimum of 15 participants is required for each course.

George Wallis
Personnel Manager

Try it for yourself! The answer appears on page 170.

Using more advanced table functions

At **Third Level**, you are asked to produce a more complex table with up to ten columns. This will require a border and some gridlines. Clear instructions will be given either at the top of the assignment, or within the table itself.

At **Third Level**, cells may need to be merged or split to achieve the required display. Some cells will also need to be shaded. The depth of shading is not given, but you must make sure that the text can be easily read.

The paper orientation for the table is landscape. It may also be necessary to reduce the font size so that the table will fit on to one page.

Exercise 5.3 (see page 41) is an example of a complex table at **Third Level**.

Try it for yourself! The time allowance for this table is 60 minutes. See if you can complete the table and print it out within the time! The correct answer appears on page 171.

Using multi-level numbering

Another advanced feature tested at **Third Level** is the use of multi-level numbering. In multi-level numbering (1, 1.1, 1.1.1, etc), text is indented so that everything with the same kind of numbering is aligned vertically. Each more detailed level of numbering (1.1, 1.1.1, etc) is indented further to the right. This successive indenting requires tabs to be set carefully. Multi-level numbering can be achieved manually or automatically, depending on the software in use. You must make sure that your version follows the given layout. You may also be asked to rearrange the order of items in the listing. The final document will be two pages in length and there will be specific instructions relating to the numbering of the pages.

Exercise 5.4 (see page 42) is an extract from a **Third Level** assignment requiring the use of multi-level numbering.

Try it for yourself! The correct version appears on page 172.

EXERCISE 5.3

Embolden underlined text

GODDINGTON PARK CONFERENCE CENTRE — increase font size and underline

SHADE THIS SECTION

MEETING ROOM INFORMATION — italic

Room Name	Palace	Shirling	Tamar	Wallace
Floor	Ground	Ground	First	First
Capacities				
theatre	130	35	45	50
classroom	70	20	20	25
boardroom	50	18	25	30
U-shape	50	20	18	24
lunch/dinner	–	–	–	–
reception	–	–	–	–
Dimensions				
length	13.29	7.63	9.15	9.76
width	11.74	7.93	9.15	9.76
area (sq m)	162	62	85.56	100
height	3.05	3.05	3.05	3.05

TECHNICAL INFORMATION — italic

Room Name	Palace	Shirling	Tamar	Wallace
Floor	Ground	Ground	First	First
Lighting				
controls in room	yes	yes	yes	yes
dimmers	yes	no	yes	yes
blackout	yes	no	yes	yes
windows	yes	no	yes	yes
Sound	yes	yes	yes	yes
Power	40	10	10	6
Access				
door height	1.98	1.98	1.98	1.98
door width	2.36	0.81	0.81	1.22
Miscellaneous				
telephone points	yes	yes	yes	no / yes
air conditioning	yes	no	no	no

Our conference accommodation is equipped with OHPs, screen, whiteboards, flipcharts, TV monitor, video recorder and slide carousel projectors.

EXERCISE 5.4

ASSIGNMENT 5 - Candidate's Copy

1   Key in the following document expanding abbreviations.
2   Use a justified right hand margin.
3   Number the second page at the bottom centre.
4   Follow any other instructions which appear within the document.
5   Proofread carefully.
6   Save your work and print out a copy on A4 portrait.

COMLON CONFERENCES PLC   — bold

MINUTES OF MEETING of the Committee held on ..✗... at 3.30 pm in Meeting Room A.   *insert today's date*

PRESENT   Stephen Knowles *(Chairman)*
               Alison Edgerley *(Secretary)*
               Geeta Chana
               Pam Williamson
               Roz Charles
               Martin Davis

               Yvonne Styles (Treasurer)

1   APOLOGIES FOR ABSENCE

    received
    Apologies were ~~presented~~ from Jed Foster.

    LAST
2   MINUTES OF ~~PREVIOUS~~ MEETING

    The Minutes of the last meeting were agreed *and signed.*

3   MATTERS ARISING

    3.1   Pam Williamson reported on negotiations with the Local Council regarding the widening of the main driveway. Copies of the ~~relevant~~ correspondence were distributed *to members.*

    3.2   Martin Davis read a letter from Voyager International, contracting to train all their new staff exclusively with Comlon. *The estimated value of the work amounted to £150,000 per annum.*

(continued)

EXERCISE 5.4 (continued)

Second paragraph for CAR PARKING

It was suggested that a new layout for the carpark might avoid some problems. A new layout would be presented at the next meeting.
Action: Martin Davis

(*)
4.2 Pam Williamson expressed concern over poor attendance on recent Time Management courses. It was agreed that the no of courses shd be reduced in an effort to improve attendance figures.
Action: Pam Williamson

5
~~4~~   CAR PARKING

restricted

Members expressed concern about the car parking currently available at the main site. On busy days, delegates encounter difficulty in parking and have on occasions had to park ~~outside~~ _on_ the main ~~driveway~~ _road_, causing complaints from local residents.

4
~~5~~   CURRICULUM DEVELOPMENT ISSUES

These have proved to be very popular and a no of new cos have expressed interest.

4
~~5~~.1   Roz Charles reported on the new modern language training modules currently being offered to local businesses at a reduced cost. It was suggested that the range of languages should be extended _as ap._

indent

Action: Roz Charles

(*)
OPEN DAY   6

initial caps

_NP_

Yvonne Styles thanked all members for their valuable help in making last month's open day a great success. Over 250 representatives from local business and commerce attended and a significant amount of new work resulted from this chance to view the conference facilities. A memo would be sent to all staff, both academic and administrative, to thank them for their efforts.

Action: Yvonne Styles

8
~~7~~   DATE OF NEXT MEETING

To be advised.

Chairman ....   Date ....

7   PUBLICITY

Concern was expressed about a new publicity campaign featuring a local training org. It was felt that this was detrimental to Comlon in that the publicity material suggested that the competitor was the only provider in the area. It was agreed to raise local awareness of Comlon by higher profile advertising.   Action: SK

HELPFUL HINTS

- Set a simple tab to align text – do not use the space bar.

- Align column headings and words and figures within columns to the left unless otherwise instructed.

- Do not worry about leaving equal space between columns.

- Do not include gridlines or borders unless specifically instructed to do so.

- Learn how to merge and split rows and columns for success at Third Level.

- Learn how to include some, but not all, gridlines within a table.

- Practise until you can achieve complex tables within the time limit of 60 minutes.

- Learn how to display text using multi-level numbering techniques.

6

Merging text

After carefully studying this chapter, you should be able to:

1 *create and use standard paragraphs;*

2 *produce a standard letter for a mail merge;*

3 *produce a data file for a mail merge;*

4 *produce merged documents;*

5 *follow instructions to move text from one document to another;*

6 *accurately size a graphic within a document.*

Extended Syllabus references

Second Level

Candidates must be able to:

6.1 Create a standard framework letter

6.2 Create a simple data file

Note: The data file should contain the date, addresses, salutation and up to 3 simple data items

6.3 Merge the framework and date file to produce a number of mail merge documents

7.1 Create a series of standard paragraphs

Note: The number of paragraphs should not exceed 10

7.2 Create a standard framework document

7.3 Add selected standard paragraphs to framework document

Third Level

Candidates must be able to:

1.1 Incorporate a graphic at a marked location

1.2 Size graphic to fit appropriately within document

13.1 Locate and define block of text in another file

13.2 Insert defined text in new working file

13.3 Insert text file in a working file

Using standard paragraphs

Assignment 4 at **Second Level** tests your ability to store and use standard paragraphs. Part 1 of Assignment 4 provides a list of up to 10 standard paragraphs which you must key in and store for later use. You do not need to produce a print-out for marking.

Part 2 gives you the layout of a standard document. You are then asked to produce 2 copies of this, each one incorporating selected paragraphs from storage.

In total, you need to produce 2 print-outs for this assignment. You have a time allowance of 30 minutes for each part.

Exercise 6.1–1 is Part 1 of Assignment 4 at Second Level.

EXERCISE 6.1–1

ASSIGNMENT 4 – PART 1 – Candidate's Copy

Key in the following paragraphs and save them so that they can be used later for boilerplating. Do not key in the numbers unless your system requires them.

1 An optional examination will take place during the final week of the course.

2 You will receive 20 hours of lessons each week.

3 Extra-curricular activities include outdoor sports and excursions to places of interest.

4 Extra-curricular activities include visits to concerts and museums.

5 You will stay with an English family who will include you in family life.

6 You may make your own accommodation arrangements but we would recommend that you live with an English family.

7 Your course will begin with an Entry Test which will take place at 9 am on the first day.

8 Fees include breakfast and dinner on weekdays and full board at weekends.

9 The College Refectory is open for lunch and dinner on weekdays but is closed at weekends.

10 Examination entries are the personal responsibility of the student.

Try it for yourself! Did you manage to key in the sentences, proofread them and save them to disk within the 30 minutes allowed?

Now on to Exercise 6.1–2, Part 2 of Assignment 4.

EXERCISE 6.1–2

ASSIGNMENT 4 – PART 2 – Candidate's Copy

The shells of two documents are given below. Key in the text as 2 separate pages. The first paragraph must be laid out as indicated.

Add to each page, in the order shown, the standard paragraphs listed.

ENGLISH LANGUAGE CENTRE

Thank you for choosing the English Language Centre. The following information refers to our Junior courses:

(Add paragraphs 2, 5, 8 and 3)

ENGLISH LANGUAGE CENTRE

Thank you for choosing the English Language Centre. The following information refers to our Adult courses:

(Add paragraphs 2, 7, 1 and 4)

Try it for yourself! You should now have keyed in the standard document, saved it to disk and then printed out 2 copies, each one incorporating the requested standard paragraphs. Check your answer on page 174.

Using mail merge

Your skill in producing mail-merged documents is tested at **Second Level**. Assignment 2 is given a time allowance of 60 minutes, and in that time you must produce a standard letter from manuscript copy, key the details into a data file, save the two files and merge them to produce 3 personalised letters. You must produce 5 print-outs for this assignment.

The standard letter is handwritten and an encircled X marks the position in the text where the standard information will later be inserted. You must choose your own field names for each item of variable information. When you have keyed in this letter, you must produce a print-out of your work for marking.

The data file information appears on the second page of the assignment and is in typescript. You must create a data file with the appropriate field names and key in the data. A print-out of this document must also be produced.

The final part of the assignment is the requirement to merge the two documents so that 3 personalised letters are produced. You must produce a copy of each of these letters for marking purposes.

Exercise 6.2 gives the standard letter for you to key in.

EXERCISE 6.2

1   Key in the following standard letter with a ragged right margin.

2   Insert merge points at the places shown with an X to take the information shown on the next page.

3   Print one copy of this shell letter.

4   Key in the information on the next page as a datafile and print one copy of the file.

5   Merge the datafile with the shell letter and print one copy of each merged letter.

JP/

Today's date

Ⓧ

Dear Ⓧ

Thank you for your cheque for Ⓧ, the final payment on your forthcoming holiday to Ⓧ. I enclose your insurance policy document and a personalised itinerary.

Your travel tickets will be forwarded to your home address approximately 14 days prior to your departure date. Please check that the names on the tickets are correct.

On behalf of Comlon Holidays we hope you have an enjoyable holiday.

Yours sincerely

Jan Percival
Reservations Manager

Encs

Try it for yourself! The correct version appears on page 175. Do not worry if your field names are different.

Exercise 6.3 gives data file details.

EXERCISE 6.3

Miss Rita Lewis	Mr John Byrne	Mrs Sarah Day
15 High Street	6 Walnut Close	3 The Avenue
COVENTRY	NOTTINGHAM	WIGSTON
CV2 8LP	NG3 9RV	LE6 2MN
Miss Lewis	Mr Byrne	Mrs Day
£1500	£800	£1950
Australia	Denmark	Malaysia

Try it for yourself! Check your answer on page 176. Your data file might not look just like this one, but the information contained within it should be identical.

Now merge the two files. You should produce 3 letters, each one containing different variable information. Did you manage to do the assignment within the 60 minutes' time allowance? If you took longer than this, keep practising until you can do it within the time.

Merging two files

At **Third Level**, you are tested on your ability to move text from one document to another. Therefore, you may be asked to take a paragraph or block of text from one assignment and import it into the assignment you are currently working on. It is very important therefore that you use meaningful file names when saving your work to disk so that the earlier assignment can be easily located and the move achieved successfully.

You will be given clear instructions telling you which block of text is to be moved. However, it is vital that all **Third Level** assignment work is saved carefully.

Importing a graphic into a document

At **Third Level**, Assignment 4 tests your ability to import a graphic into a piece of continuous text. The graphic is not specified, but you should choose a graphic which fits in with the topic of the document. For example, if the subject matter of the text is about travel, then a suitable graphic might be an aeroplane, a boat or a car.

You will, however, be given specific instructions relating to the position and the sizing of the graphic. As with any measurements, the size of the graphic will be expressed in centimetres or millimetres and in inches. You will incur a penalty if your graphic does not measure exactly the size given. You will be instructed whether or not to place a border around the graphic. You must follow all instructions carefully.

Exercise 6.4 will help you to practise importing a graphic into a document and sizing it appropriately.

EXERCISE 6.4

1 Key in the text below, following instructions.
2 Use a fully justified right margin.
3 Size and position the graphic as instructed.
4 Centre the text vertically on the page.
5 Proof-read carefully and print out a copy of your work.

COMLON BOOKS — bold and centre

Welcome to Comlon Books — a unique book club that always gives you, the reader, the freedom to choose ~~all~~ the books you want, when you want them. We offer high quality books at reduced prices, often as much as 50% less than the recommended retail price;

insert a suitable graphic here measuring 50 cm (2 inches) across by 3.8 cm (1.5 inches) deep. Use a border.

run on Not only that, if you are not delighted with your choice, we offer a unique service which enables you to ~~&~~ return the book for a full refund.

All books featured will be at a reduced ~~rate~~ price.

YOUR COMMITMENT — bold
All we ask of our ~~customers~~ members is that they purchase 3 books within the first 12 months of membership. Each month an order form will accompany the Comlon ~~booklet~~ Newsletter. You should make your choice and place your order within 10
uc days of receipt of the ~~newsletter~~ newsletter. Your books will be delivered within 48 hours.

PAYMENT — bold
Payment should accompany each order. In the unlikely case of a book being returned to us, we will credit your account immed. All payments and credits will be shown on your monthly statement. Payment can be made by cheque or credit card.

(continued)

EXERCISE 6.4 (continued)

DATA PROTECTION ACT — bold

Comlon Books [always operates within the terms and spirit of the
D— P— Act. We are registered with the Data Protection
Registrar. Occasionally we make lists of members' names
and addresses available to companies whose products or
services we feel may be of interest. Please let us know
if you do not wish to receive such mailings.

HOW THE CLUB WORKS — bold

INSERT THIS PARAGRAPH
AS PARAGRAPH NUMBER
TWO

Newsletter

Each month we will send you our Comlon Newsletter
which gives details of the titles which are currently
available for sale. A review accompanies each listing.
All books have been especially selected by our editorial
team to ensure that you have access to some of the
best writers and their works.

HAPPY READING! — bold and centre

Try it for yourself! Does your version look like the one which appears on
page 177? You may have chosen a different graphic, but as long as the
size is correct, there will be no penalty.

HELPFUL HINTS

- Remember to save your standard paragraphs under sensible file names.

- Check that the standard paragraphs are used in the specified order.

- Use sensible field names for the variable information in your standard letter.

- Make sure that your data file contains all the necessary information.

- Remember that 5 print-outs are needed for this mail-merge assignment.

- Sensible file names will enable you to find your work easily and quickly.

- Choose a graphic which is appropriate to the subject matter of the document.

- Learn how to size your graphic accurately.

- Follow instructions relating to borders around your graphic.

7

Advanced features

After carefully studying this chapter, you should be able to:

1 *produce a form from handwritten copy;*

2 *use newspaper columns to display your work attractively;*

3 *use footnotes within a multi-page document.*

Extended Syllabus references

Second Level

Candidates must be able to:

10.1   Design a form intended for completion by hand

10.2   Allocate appropriate space for completing each item

Third Level

Candidates must be able to:

10.1   Insert footnotes at appropriate position within document

11.1   Include text in columns within a document

11.2   Wrap text around a graphic box

Producing a form

Assignment 5b at **Second Level** tests your ability to produce a form from handwritten copy. The form must fit on to one page of A4 portrait, and you must leave sufficient space for it to be completed by hand. Therefore, it is vital that you use double line spacing for the production of the form.

You will be required to use rows of dots at entry points. Some rows will be continuous, but others will be short rows requiring just one word or number or a tick for completion. Remember to leave at least one space after the text before starting the rows of dots.

You will find the form easier to produce if you know how to set simple tabs and leader dots within your software. You are allowed 30 minutes in which to complete and print out the form.

Exercise 7.1 is a typical example of a form at **Second Level**.

EXERCISE 7.1

ASSIGNMENT 5 - PART 2 - Candidate's Copy

Create a form with the headings shown. As the form will be completed by hand, leave enough space for each of the entries.

COMLON TRAINING PLC
APPLICATION FORM } bold

Please complete and return this form to Comlon Training PLC, Warwick Chambers, Granby Place, Leicester LE6 4HP.

DELEGATE DETAILS

Full Name . . . .
Home Address . . . .
. . . .
Postcode . . . . Telephone . . . .

COMPANY DETAILS

Company Name . . . .
Address . . . .
. . . . Postcode . . . . . .
Telephone . . . . Fax . . . .

COURSE DETAILS

Course Title . . . .
Preferred Dates (1) . . . .
(2) . . . .
(3) . . . .

I enclose a cheque for £50 made payable to Comlon Training PLC. I understand that this deposit is refundable only in the event of the course being cancelled.

SIGNATURE . . . . DATE . . . .

Try it for yourself! If it took you more than 30 minutes to produce a copy identical to the one shown on page 178, practise until you can complete the task within the time allowance.

Using newspaper columns

Using newspaper columns is a **Third Level** function which tests your ability to display work attractively in columns. The document will require the use of a centred heading in a large font size surrounded by a border. The text will be displayed in two columns. The document must fit on one page. All margins must be fully justified.

Exercise 7.2 is an example of a **Third Level** assignment using columns.

EXERCISE 7.2

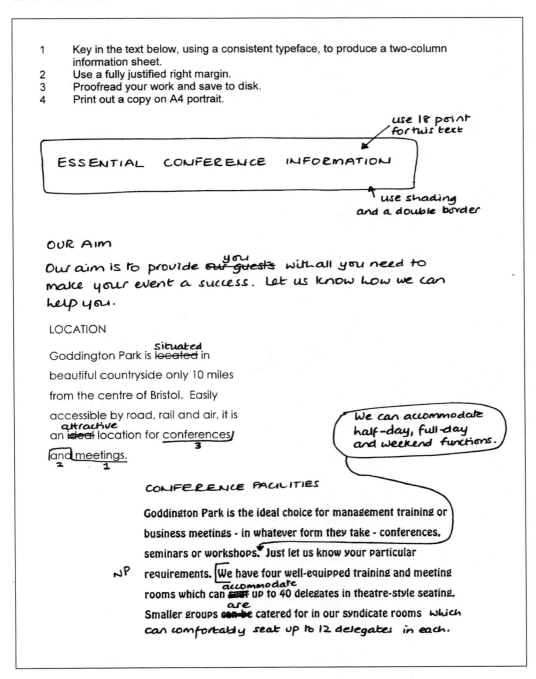

1. Key in the text below, using a consistent typeface, to produce a two-column information sheet.
2. Use a fully justified right margin.
3. Proofread your work and save to disk.
4. Print out a copy on A4 portrait.

use 18 point for this text

ESSENTIAL CONFERENCE INFORMATION

use shading and a double border

OUR AIM

Our aim is to provide ~~our guests~~ you with all you need to make your event a success. Let us know how we can help you.

LOCATION

Goddington Park is ~~located~~ situated in beautiful countryside only 10 miles from the centre of Bristol. Easily accessible by road, rail and air, it is an ~~ideal~~ attractive location for conferences and meetings.

We can accommodate half-day, full-day and weekend functions.

CONFERENCE FACILITIES

Goddington Park is the ideal choice for management training or business meetings - in whatever form they take - conferences, seminars or workshops. Just let us know your particular requirements. We have four well-equipped training and meeting rooms which can ~~seat~~ accommodate up to 40 delegates in theatre-style seating. Smaller groups ~~can be~~ are catered for in our syndicate rooms which can comfortably seat up to 12 delegates in each.

(continued)

EXERCISE 7.2 (continued)

NP [Each meeting room is equipped with television, video, overhead projector and flipchart. Desktop projection equipment is available on request.

RESIDENTIAL
~~OVERNIGHT~~ FACILITIES

Goddington Park is a residential centre ~~which offers~~ *offering* all the comforts of a country *and benefits* house. There are 25 study bedrooms located on the first and second floors.

All have their own distinctive character and most overlook the ~~rear~~ gardens. A lift serves both floors.

Each room has a private bathroom with shower, wc and washbasin. There is a television and a hair dryer in each room. Tea and coffee making facilities are / *also* provided.

Food and Drink

A large, airy restaurant overlooking the gardens is open to delegates ~~during~~ *throughout* their stay. Our resident chef can offer a wide range of menu options. Let us know your preferences in advance and we will be pleased to supply you with sample menus.

RELAXATION

To relax after a busy day, Goddington Park offers a ~~full~~ range of activities – croquet, tennis, table-tennis, billiards and even a fitness suite / *with exercise equipment* ,
A small indoor swimming pool aids relaxation.

Try it for yourself! The correct answer appears on page 179.

Using footnotes

Your ability to use footnotes is tested in a **Third Level** assignment, and for this you must be able to identify the key words with a reference symbol or number (as shown in the manuscript copy) and produce the footnote at the bottom of the same page. No more than 3 footnotes will be incorporated into the assignment. Your footnotes may appear with or without a line that separates them from the main part of the document.

Try Exercise 7.3, a **Third Level** assignment which incorporates the use of footnotes.

EXERCISE 7.3

1   Key in the following text and edit as shown.
2   Repaginate sensibly and number each page at the bottom centre.
3   Use a justified right-hand margin.
4   Insert footnotes as appropriate.
5   Proofread your work carefully and save to disk.
6   Print a copy on A4 paper.

ARRANGE ITEMS IN ORDER INDICATED BUT DO NOT NUMBER

STRESS AT WORK   — bold and centre

this paragraph in double line spacing

①   *acknowledged*
The workplace is generally ~~thought~~ to be one of the major sources of stress for many people. As most of us spend more time at work than we do at home, it is inevitable that *difficult* working conditions can lead to feelings of stress.

②   However, work also offers many opportunities to channel stress towards positive ends. A stimulating and challenging job ~~role~~ can provide the means by which an individual can forget about problems in other areas of life.

⑤   Environmental Stress   – bold

poor security and

Many employees work in a stressful environment, where poor light, inadequate ventilation, overcrowding, drab surroundings often combine to depress even the most optimistic worker. The company is duty-bound by law[1] to ensure that basic standards are met and employees should draw problems to the attention of management.

④   External Pressures

Many jobs are directly subjected to external pressures — meeting an urgent order, making a presentation to a major client, dealing with the general public — and an individual can experience strong feelings of insecurity on a daily basis.

1 The Health and Safety at Work Act 1974

(continued)

EXERCISE 7.3 (continued)

⑥ SOME SOLUTIONS   — bold

Here are some suggestions which might improve the stress at work:

⑦ Communication   — bold

Ordinary work problems ~~are~~ *will be* defused if you can talk about them. Try to involve ~~others~~ your family, trustworthy colleagues and friends and acquaintances who work in similar jobs. In this way potentially stressful situations can be avoided.

Ideally, you should aim to talk ~~to~~ directly to your line manager.

⑧ Change and Uncertainty

Much stress is brought about by changes in the workplace. A merger or take-over, a major reorganisation, changing work patterns — all of these can cause employees to suffer from stress. It is the feeling of insecurity that fuels the stress and this is often made worse by poor communication.

⑨ Feedback

Try to make sure that you receive regular feedback on your performance from the person to whom you are answerable. In this way you will be alerted before any minor concerns become major issues.

⑩ Physical Conditions   (Do all you can)

~~Try~~ to make sure that your personal working environment is efficient and comfortable. If you work at a desk or a computer, check that your seating is suitable[2], that your VDU is glare-free and that you have adequate space in which to perform your job.

---

[2] Display Screen & Equipment Regulations 1992

(continued)

EXERCISE 7.3 (continued)

⑧ Forward Planning

Whilst all stressful situations cannot be avoided, sensible forward planning can ensure that you are not forced into last-minute actions. Use checklists for regular events, prepare well in advance of meetings and try to use your time effectively.

⑪ By making a few simple changes to your work patterns, you will find that you can eliminate some stress from your working life.

Check your answer with the correct version which appears on pages 180–181.

HELPFUL HINTS

- Learn to set simple tabs and leader dots for easy production of the form.

- It is a good idea to key in the text first before formatting for newspaper columns.

- Try to align the top headings within the column area.

- Make sure that the footnote appears on the same page as the footnote reference.

- You do not need to use a dividing line to separate the footnotes from the remainder of the document.

8

Marking criteria

After carefully studying this chapter, you should be able to:

1 *understand how your work is marked;*

2 *understand what constitutes an error;*

3 *appreciate the need for careful proofreading;*

4 *avoid making the commonest types of errors.*

How your work is marked

When each assignment is complete, it will be marked by your tutor. Your tutor will use a marking copy provided by the LCCI Examinations Board. Your work will be compared with the correct version and any errors will be circled. The total number of errors made will determine the grade you receive for the assignment. If you fail one assignment in the set, you may retake the corresponding assignment from the reserve set. You may not retake more than one failed assignment. You must pass every assignment to gain an overall Pass grade.

What is an error?

An error is any uncorrected mistake which appears in your work. It could be any of the following:

- a keyboarding error or misspelled word
- an omitted word
- an extra word
- failure to embolden, centre or underline a heading
- failure to change margins
- failure to change line spacing
- failure to include page numbers, etc.

In fact, the list could be endless. Every time you do not do what is asked of you in the assignment instructions, you will incur an error. Your tutor will circle the mistake in ink on your document and give you an appropriate grade. When you have completed the whole set of assignments, your work is then sent to the LCCI Examinations Board where a moderator will re-mark your work to ensure that your work has been accurately marked and graded by your tutor.

In the majority of cases, the candidates' work has been accurately marked, and moderators will not change the grades. However, the moderator can change grades if it is felt that the work has not been marked according to the marking scheme.

Examples of marked work

On the following pages, you will see some examples of work which have been marked by a tutor. The three candidates involved have produced work which contains errors; however, candidate A achieves a good pass, candidate B achieves a borderline pass and candidate C fails the assignment.

This is the **First Level** assignment which they were given:

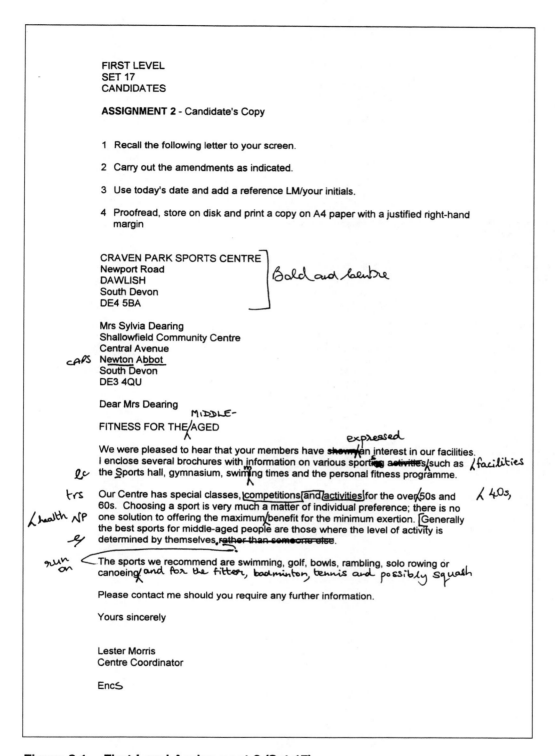

Figure 8.1   First Level Assignment 2 (Set 17)

The marking scheme supplied by the LCCI Examinations Board demands that their work looks like Figure 8.2 (page 64).

CRAVEN PARK SPORTS CENTRE
Newport Road
DAWLISH
South Devon
DE4 5BA

LM/RBL

Today's date

Mrs Sylvia Dearing
Shallowfield Community Centre
Central Avenue
NEWTON ABBOT
South Devon
DE3 4QU

Dear Mrs Dearing

FITNESS FOR THE MIDDLE-AGED

We were pleased to hear that your members have expressed an interest in our facilities. I enclose several brochures with information on various sports facilities such as the sports hall, gymnasium, swimming times and the personal fitness programme.

Our Centre has special classes, activities and competitions for the over 40s, 50s and 60s. Choosing a sport is very much a matter of individual preference; there is no one solution to offering the maximum health benefit for the minimum exertion.

Generally the best sports for middle-aged people are those where the level of activity is determined by themselves. The sports we recommend are swimming, golf, bowls, rambling, solo rowing or canoeing and for the fitter, badminton, tennis and possibly squash.

Please contact me should you require any further information.

Yours sincerely

Lester Morris
Centre Coordinator

Encs

Figure 8.2   Model Answer to First Level Assignment 2 (Set 17)

Figures 8.3, 8.4 and 8.5 show the work produced by the candidates.

CANDIDATE A

CRAVEN PARK SPORTS CENTRE
Newport Road
DAWLISH
South Devon
DE4 5BA

LM/RBL

Mrs Sylvia Dearing
Shallowfield Community Centre
Central Avenue
NEWTON ABBOT
South Devon
DE3 4QU

3 March [year]

Dear Mrs Dearing

FITNESS FOR THE MIDDLE-AGED

We were pleased to hear that your members have expressed an interest in our facilities. I enclose several brochures with information on various sports facilities such as the sports hall, gymnasium, swimming times and the personal fitness programme.

Our Centre has special classes, activities and competitions for the over 40s, 50s and 60s. Choosing a sport is very much a matter of individual preference; there is no one solution to offering the maximum health benefit for the minimum exertion.

Generally the best sports for middle-aged people are those where the level of activity is determined by themselves.

① The sports we recommend are swimming, golf, bowls, rambling, solo rowing or canoeing and for the fitter, badminton, tennis and possibly squash.

Please contact me should you require any further information.

Yours sincerely

Lester Morris
Centre Coordinator

Encs

Figure 8.3   Candidate A's answer to First Level Assignment 2 (Set 17)

CANDIDATE B

CRAVEN PARK SPORTS CENTRE
Newport Road
DAWLISH
South Devon
DE4 5BA

LM/JP

3 March   ①

Mrs Sylvia Dearing
Shallowfield Community Centre
Central Avenue
NEWTON ABBOT
South Devon
DE3 4QU

Dear Mrs Dearing

FITNESS FOR THE MIDDLE-AGED

We were pleased to hear that your members have expressed an interest in our   ②
facilities. I enclose several brochures with information on various sports facilities
such as the sports hall, gymnasium, swimming times and the personal fitness
programme.

Our Centre has special classes, activities and competitions for the over 40s, 50s
and 60s. Choosing a sport is very much a matter of individual preference; there is
no one solution to offering the maximum health benefit for the minimum exertion.

Generally the best sports for middle-aged people are those where the level of
activity is determined by themselves. The sports we recommend are swimming,
golf, bowls, rambling, solo rowing or canoeing and for the fitter, badminton, tenis   ③
and possibly squash.

Please contact me should you require any further information.

Yours sincerely

Lester Morris
Centre Coordinator

Encs

Figure 8.4   Candidate B's answer to First Level Assignment 2 (Set 17)

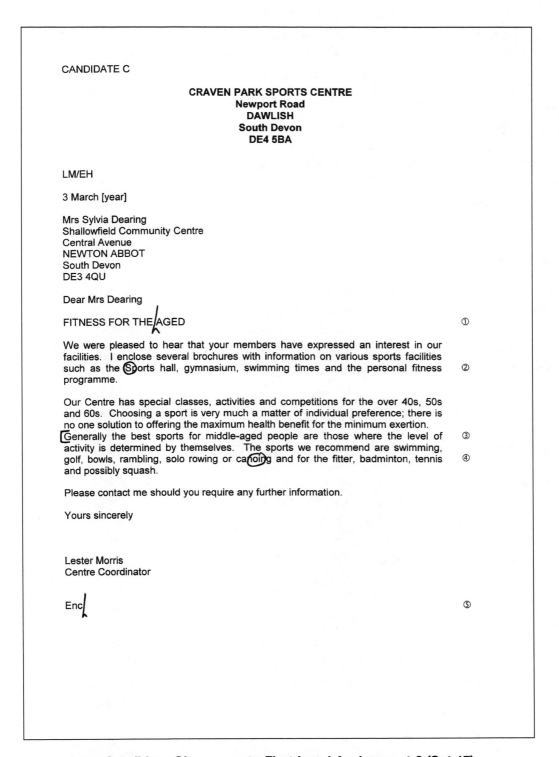

CANDIDATE C

CRAVEN PARK SPORTS CENTRE
Newport Road
DAWLISH
South Devon
DE4 5BA

LM/EH

3 March [year]

Mrs Sylvia Dearing
Shallowfield Community Centre
Central Avenue
NEWTON ABBOT
South Devon
DE3 4QU

Dear Mrs Dearing

FITNESS FOR THE AGED ①

We were pleased to hear that your members have expressed an interest in our facilities. I enclose several brochures with information on various sports facilities such as the Sports hall, gymnasium, swimming times and the personal fitness ② programme.

Our Centre has special classes, activities and competitions for the over 40s, 50s and 60s. Choosing a sport is very much a matter of individual preference; there is no one solution to offering the maximum health benefit for the minimum exertion. Generally the best sports for middle-aged people are those where the level of ③ activity is determined by themselves. The sports we recommend are swimming, golf, bowls, rambling, solo rowing or canoing and for the fitter, badminton, tennis ④ and possibly squash.

Please contact me should you require any further information.

Yours sincerely

Lester Morris
Centre Coordinator

Enc ⑤

Figure 8.5   Candidate C's answer to First Level Assignment 2 (Set 17)

Let us have a closer look at each candidate's work.

Candidate A

This candidate made only one error. This was the failure to join paragraphs 3 and 4. The rest of the assignment was error-free.

Note, however, that Candidate A did not position the date underneath the reference. This is not an error. The candidate can choose where to position the date. However, if the date were omitted or incomplete, that would be an error.

Candidate B

This candidate was less accurate than Candidate A but produced work which was good enough to pass. The errors were an incomplete date (1), failure to justify the right margin (2) and one keyboarding or spelling error (3).

Candidate C

This candidate did not proofread his or her work and therefore produced an assignment which contained too many errors to pass. The errors included an omitted word (middle) (1), failure to change an initial capital to lower case (sports) (2), failure to leave a clear line space between paragraphs 3 and 4 (3), a keyboarding or spelling error (canoeing) (4), and the omission of the final 's' on 'Encs' (5).

How to be successful in your assignments

It is always disappointing to fail an assignment. Candidates are demotivated by failure, and tutors and moderators do not enjoy marking work which does not reach the required standard. To avoid this happening to you, let us consider why some candidates fail. Here are some simple steps which you can take to ensure your success.

1 Proofread your work very carefully

Many candidates simply do not check their work carefully enough. They rely too heavily on the spellchecker on their computer and do not spend time checking their word-processed work against the original instruction sheet. The spellchecker will identify many keyboarding or spelling errors but it will not identify omitted or extra words which will become errors.

It is imperative, therefore, to check your work very carefully before handing it to your tutor for marking. Use the spellchecker, but also check your work by proofreading it yourself.

2 Practise the functions to be tested until you are fully competent

Many candidates attempt an assignment before they are sufficiently competent in the function to be tested. They may have practised the function once or twice, but have not had to produce an assignment within a specified time. Therefore, if they get into difficulty, they are too inexperienced to solve their problems.

You should not attempt an assignment until you feel that you can confidently undertake all the tasks required of you. This is the major advantage of Practical Word Processing assignments. You can choose when you take the assignments. You should only take the assignments when *you* are ready.

3 Read the instructions carefully

Many candidates fail an assignment simply because they have failed to carry out all the instructions contained within it. They may have forgotten to insert page numbers on all pages or have failed to make a line spacing or margin change. In all cases, the instruction would have appeared clearly on the assignment.

At **First** and **Second Levels**, most of the instructions are listed at the top of the assignment sheet in a numbered list. It is a good idea to tick each instruction off as you complete it. At **Third Level**, many instructions are included within the assignment itself. Once again, tick each instruction off as you complete it. In this way there is less chance of overlooking an instruction and thereby failing an assignment.

4 Practise on past assignments

The best type of practice for an examination is a past examination paper. Therefore, it is unwise to attempt a set of Practical Word Processing assignments if you have had no prior experience of doing a set of past assignments. Only by practising the assignments within the specified time allowance will you get a clear idea of what is asked of you. At the end of this book, there is a set of assignments at each of the three levels. Try them for yourself and check your answers with the marking copy provided.

5 Know your limitations

It is always disappointing for tutors and moderators to mark work which is clearly not up to the required standard purely because the candidate does not possess the skills necessary for the level of assignments undertaken.

First Level assignments can be achieved by candidates with a basic knowledge of word processing and a slow but accurate keyboarding skill. **Second Level** assignments require a greater level of keyboarding skill and the amount of text to be keyed in by the candidate demands a higher speed. **Third Level** assignments, by their very nature, are both demanding and complex, and require a high level of keyboarding competence on the part of the candidate.

It is important that you know your own limitations and seek to progress only as and when your keyboarding competence and speed allow.

9

Practice assignments

This chapter contains a set of assignments at **First, Second** and **Third Levels**. These assignments will enable you to practise putting your word-processing skills to the test under timed conditions.

Before you begin the assignments, you will need to key in and save to disk some documents that you will later recall and amend. I have given you specific file names under which to store your documents. This will ensure that you will recall the correct document for the assignments.

However, when you take your assignments in your word-processing class, your tutor will give you file names which are more appropriate to your particular system.

There are 3 assignments to be keyed in for the **First Level** assignments. There is one assignment to be keyed in at each of **Second** and **Third Levels**. These tutor inputs appear on the following pages.

When working through the assignments, follow the instructions at the top of each assignment carefully. Try to work within the time allowance allocated for each assignment. In this way you can assess whether or not you are ready to attempt a set of Practical Word Processing assignments and gain a formal qualification in word processing.

Good luck!

Tutor inputs

FIRST LEVEL
SET 19
TUTORS

ASSIGNMENT 2 – Tutor's Input

Note to Tutor: Enter this text exactly as shown here, including formatting, page breaks and any deliberate errors and save as [PWP1ASS2] for use by candidates.

THE RELATIVES ASSOCIATION
200 Chiswell Street
LONDON
EC2Y 3BU

Mrs R Curtis
125 Windmill Road
Cheshunt
Herts
EN7 4SP

Dear Mrs Curtis

THE RELATIVES ASSOCIATION

Thank you for your enquiry into our Association. Further details about our services are provided in the leaflet attached.

The Association is now a registered charity and is given a grant from the Department of Health.

The Relatives Association tries to achieve the best possible standards of care both at home and in nursing homes. It was founded in 1992 by a group of people who all found they had experienced similar problems when an elderly relative needed care at home or in a nursing home.

Sometimes the need for a relative to move into a home has been sudden. Quite often a decision has been reached after a long period of care by a husband or wife. In any event the decision is often very difficult.

The Relatives Association recognises these problems and is there to help sort out any aspects of concern.

Yours sincerely

Belinda Reeves
Association Secretary

FIRST LEVEL
SET 19
TUTORS

ASSIGNMENT 4 – Tutor's Input

Note to Tutor: Enter this text exactly as shown here, including formatting, page breaks and any deliberate errors and save as [PWP1ASS4] for use by candidates.

MEMORANDUM

To   P Walters, Senior Officer

From   Belinda Reeves, Association Secretary

Ref

Date

In giving advice to our clients we first investigate other sources of help.
These include Local Authorities and private nursing organisations. In addition
there are voluntary organisations and charitable trusts. All can provide care
by skilled staff 24 hours a day.

Ensure that you point out that a residential care home is not a nursing home.
People who need nursing care will need the additional support of the District
Nursing Service. In their investigations remind your staff that when people
go into a home it should feel just like going into their own homes.

It should provide a homely environment and meet the needs of the individual.

Above all the purpose of such care is to enable people to live enjoyable,
independent and fulfilled lives as far as possible.

FIRST LEVEL
SET 19
TUTORS

ASSIGNMENT 6 – Tutor's Input

Note to Tutor: Enter this text exactly as shown here, including formatting, page breaks and any deliberate errors and save as [PWP1ASS6] for use by candidates.

RELATIVES ASSOCIATION MEETING

Minutes of the meeting held on ... at 200 Chiswell Street, London, EC2Y 3BU at 1400.

PRESENT   Belinda Reeves (Chairman)
                     Paula Walter
                     Rita Jones
                     Hilary Edwards

APOLOGIES FOR ABSENCE

No apologies for absence were received.

MINUTES OF PREVIOUS MEETING

The minutes of the last meeting were approved and signed.

SECOND LEVEL
SET O
TUTORS

ASSIGNMENT 1 – Tutor's Input

Note to Tutors: Enter this text exactly as shown here, including formatting, page breaks and any deliberate errors. Save as [PWP2ASS1] for use by candidates.

COMLON COMPUTER TRAINING

COURSE PROGRAMME

Comlon Computer Training offers a wide selection of courses for students of all ages and abilities. Whether you are a complete beginner, or already have extensive computing skills, we offer courses at all levels to suit your particular needs.

Our courses run throughout the year too, so you, the client, can choose the timing of your training to suit your individual needs. We also have three sites – our Head Office in Central London, and two satellite branches in Canterbury and Tonbridge. So if you are located in the South East of England, we have a branch near you.

Page 2

Advanced Training

Our advanced courses are designed for users who are already comfortable with producing simple documents or artwork, and who now wish to explore the full potential of the software.

Page 3

On-Site Training

Sometimes it is more appropriate to deliver our training on the customer's own site. This may be a more cost effective option for the organisation and, for the students, learning may be more effective when carried out in a familiar environment.

THIRD LEVEL
SPECIMEN
TUTORS

ASSIGNMENT 3 – Tutor's Input

Note to Tutors: Enter this text exactly as shown here, including formatting, page breaks and any deliberate errors. Save as [PWP3ASS3] for use by candidates.

CHINA

General Information

Population: 1 billion
Area: 3,695,500 square miles
Currency: Chinese Yuan

Distance from UK: 5053 miles

Page 2

HEALTH REQUIREMENTS

The following vaccinations are recommended for all parts of China:

Polio
Typhoid
Yellow fever
Malaria
Hepatitis

First Level assignments

**EXAMINATIONS
BOARD**

**PRACTICAL WORD PROCESSING
FIRST LEVEL**

SET 19 – CANDIDATES

Candidates MUST either write or key-in their names on each printout.

These Assignments are to be used for candidate's final assessment during 1997

FIRST LEVEL
SET 19
CANDIDATES

TIME ALLOWANCE

ASSIGNMENT 1   30 minutes

                2   30 minutes

                3   30 minutes

                4   30 minutes

                5   30 minutes

                6   30 minutes

TOTAL = 3 hours

FIRST LEVEL
SET 19
CANDIDATES

ASSIGNMENT 1 - Candidate's Copy

1 Key-in the following text.

2 Add your name at the bottom left.

3 Proofread your work and print a copy on A4 paper with a justified right-hand margin.

SERVICES FOR THOSE WHO ARE SICK OR ELDERLY

The care services through which elderly or sick people can obtain help meet an important need. That is why it is so necessary to provide a complete directory of home care services and nursing homes where people can stay. It can provide information on the many different kinds of places available and will also offer useful advice on what to consider before any decision is made.

It is important that anyone thinking about moving into such a place should have the best possible information in order to choose wisely. Those having to make a choice on behalf of relatives have a more difficult task and must seek other advice as well.

FIRST LEVEL
SET 19
CANDIDATES

ASSIGNMENT 2 - Candidate's Copy

1 Recall the following letter to your screen.

2 Carry out the amendments as indicated.

3 Use today's date and add a reference BR/your initials.

4 Proofread, store on disk and print a copy on A4 paper with a justified right-hand margin

THE RELATIVES ASSOCIATION
200 Chiswell Street
LONDON
EC2Y 3BU

centre and bold

Mrs R Curtis
125 Windmill Road
Cheshunt   *CAPS*
Herts
EN7 4SP

Dear Mrs Curtis

THE RELATIVES ASSOCIATION

Thank you for your enquiry into/ *regarding* our Association. Further details about our services are provided in the leaflet attached.   *tas*

The Association is now a registered charity and is given a grant from the Department of Health. *Fund raising is still necessary* however.

The Relatives Association tries to achieve the best possible standards of care both at home and in nursing homes. It was founded in 1992 by a group of people who all found they had experienced similar problems when an elderly relative needed care at home or in a nursing home.   *moved into*

Sometimes the need for a relative to/move into a home has been sudden. Quite *son or daughter* often a decision has been reached after a long period of care by a husband, or wife. In any event the decision is often very difficult.   *be cared for at home or*

The Relatives Association recognises these problems and is there to help sort out any aspects of concern. *Our officers may be called upon when trouble strikes.*

Yours sincerely

to be cared for

Belinda Reeves
Association Secretary

Enc

FIRST LEVEL
SET 19
CANDIDATES

ASSIGNMENT 3 - Candidate's Copy

1 Key-in the following text and retain the line-spacing.

2 Centre each line and amend where indicated.

3 Keep the line-endings as shown.

4 Add your name at the bottom left.

5 Proofread, store on disk and print a copy on A4 paper.

Embolden COMLON HOMECARE each time it appears

COMLON HOMECARE
centre and bold
A HELPING HAND

COMLON HOMECARE provides a range of
flexible, individual care services as required,
24 hours a day,
all year round.

*

* Leave 2 clear line-spaces at these points.

This enables people of any age or disability
to live as normal a life as possible
in the comfort and security of their own homes.

*

To fulfil the needs of clients,
COMLON HOMECARE provides:

*

*   Personal/care *and social*

*   Practical support

*   Other related home care services

*   Community/monitoring service *alarm and*

*   1 to 24 hour cover

*

For further details *on a visit from one of our officers*
contact your local COMLON HOMECARE branch
01845 284401

FIRST LEVEL
SET 19
CANDIDATES

ASSIGNMENT 4 - Candidate's Copy

1 Recall the following memo to your screen and carry out the amendments as indicated.

2 Use today's date and add the reference BR/your initials

3 Add the heading DIFFERENT TYPES OF CARE HOMES

4 Proofread, store on disk and print a copy on A4 paper with a ragged right-hand margin.

MEMORANDUM

To   P Walters, Senior Officer

From   Belinda Reeves, Association Secretary

Ref

Date

In giving /advice to our clients /we first investigate other sources of help. These /will include Local Authorities and private nursing organisations. In addition there are voluntary organisations and charitable trusts. All can provide care by skilled staff 24 hours a day.

Ensure that /you point out that a residential care home is not a nursing home. People who need nursing care will need the additional support of the District Nursing Service. In their investigations remind your staff that when people go into a home it should feel just like going into their own homes.

It should provide a homely environment and meet the needs of the individual. Also it should promote dignity, independence and continued personal development.

Above all the purpose of such care is to enable people to live enjoyable, independent and fulfilled lives as far as possible.

[Handwritten annotations: "help and", "your staff must", "they inform clients", "either in a home or by home nursing care"]

FIRST LEVEL
SET 19
CANDIDATES

ASSIGNMENT 5 - Candidate's Copy

1 Key-in the following text with a ragged right margin.

2 Carry out the amendments indicated.

3 Proofread, store on disk and print a copy on A4 paper.

All headings in caps with one clear line-space after

MOVING INTO A CARE HOME ← *centre and bold*

it is time to move to

If you are thinking/~~of moving to~~ a Care Home you are faced with some very
important decisions and choices. You will need information about the choices
available t~~o you~~ and guidance about the questions you may wish to ask/ *before reaching a* *decision*

Bold + caps.

It would be useful to use the following as a (checklist) to help you make your decision.

CONDITIONS
Can you retain your room if away and is it possible to have a short stay or trial
t/c period? Will you be given a statement of (conditions) and (terms) on admission?

before signing an agreement

FEES
and
l.c. How much are the fees?/ What do the fees include? i.e./services and consumables
Do they include
such as toiletries? Under what circumstances will fees alter eg annually,/care
or according *to*
needs?

Accommodation ~~and Catering~~
and video
Are there communal sitting rooms with/without TV? Will you have to share a
bedroom or bathroom and if so with how many other residents? Is there adequate
wheelchair access indoors and outdoors; ~~and~~ are handrails provided in hallways
and corridors?

Transport
Is the home easy to get to for relatives and friends and how close is it to community
facilities? Does the home provide its own transport? *and do residents pay extra for this*

CATERING

Is there a choice of menu at each meal and are special
requirements catered for ie vegetarians, diabetics?

FIRST LEVEL
SET 19
CANDIDATES
ASSIGNMENT 6 - Candidate's Copy

1 Recall the following Minutes and make the necessary amendments.

2 Key-in from paragraph 3 to 8 in number order, but do not type the numbers.

3 Proofread, store on disk and print a copy on A4 paper with a justified right-hand margin.

RELATIVES ASSOCIATION MEETING ← *Bold*

Insert today's date here

Minutes of the meeting held on .. at 200 Chiswell Street, London, EC2Y 3BU at 1400.

Chairperson

PRESENT   Belinda Reeves (~~Chairman~~)
               Paula Walter
               Rita Jones
               Hilary Edwards

(1) APOLOGIES FOR ABSENCE

No apologies for absence were received.

③ *MATTERS ARISING*
There were no matters arising.

(2) MINUTES OF PREVIOUS MEETING

The minutes of the last meeting were approved and signed.

(4) RECRUITING *OF* OFFICERS

Paula Walter reported that the recruitment of officers *was* progressing well. She *was* looking for suitable applicants ~~who are~~ very experienced in the field. Interviews ∧ *of care services* start next week.

(6) RENEWAL OF CHARITY REGISTRATION

The Association is to

reported
Belinda Reeves ~~confirmed~~ that the confirmation for renewal had been received and *that* our Registered Charity No *was* 1920000. ~~We are to~~ receive a grant from the Department of Health. ∧

(5) TRAINING COURSES

Officers will be invited to attend a training course for letter writing and telephone skills to be held next month. Hilary Edwards will be making the ~~necessary~~ arrangements.

(7) ANY OTHER BUSINESS

stated
more
Belinda Reeves ~~advised~~ that the Association was receiving ~~more and more~~ details from *∧* home care establishments. These should ~~not~~ be ~~investigated~~ *∧ looked into carefully* before being offered to clients.

(8) DATE OF NEXT MEETING

NP [*The Association regretted the resignation of Rita Jones who would be moving to Scotland and thanked her for her excellent services.*

To be advised.

Second Level assignments

**PRACTICAL WORD PROCESSING
SECOND LEVEL**

SET O – CANDIDATES

Candidates MUST either write or key-in their names on each printout.

These Assignments are to be used for candidate's final assessment during 1997

SECOND LEVEL
SET O
CANDIDATES

TIME ALLOWANCE

ASSIGNMENT	1		1 hour
	2		1 hour
	3		1 hour
	4	Part 1	30 minutes
		Part 2	30 minutes
	5	Part 1	30 minutes
		Part 2	30 minutes
	6		30 minutes

TOTAL = 5 hours 30 minutes

Practice assignments

SECOND LEVEL
SET O
CANDIDATES

ASSIGNMENT 1 - Candidate's Copy

1 Recall the following document to your screen, saved under   and edit as
   shown.

2 Repaginate sensibly and number each page at the bottom.

3 Leave at least 25 mm (1") between each section.

4 Change the left margin to 50 mm (2") and the right margin to 38 mm (1½"). Give
   a fully justified right hand margin.

5 Insert a header SHORT COURSES at the top right of each page.

underline — COMLON COMPUTER TRAINING ⎞ *bold and centre*
            INFORMATION
COURSE ~~PROGRAMME~~ ⎠

                       range

Comlon Computer Training offers a wide ~~selection~~ of courses for students of all
ages and abilities. Whether you are a complete beginner, or already have
extensive computing skills, we offer courses at all levels to suit your particular
needs.

run on Our courses run throughout the year too, so you, the client, can choose the timing
of your training to suit your individual needs. We also have three sites - our Head
Office in Central London, and two satellite branches in Canterbury and Tonbridge.
~~So if you are located in the South East of England, we have a branch near you~~.

Introductory Courses   — *bold and underline*

These courses are designed for users with little or no experience
of the software package. No previous knowledge is assumed,
but it is helpful to have basic keyboarding skills. All of the
basic functions of the software package are covered, and
consolidation exercises ensure that learning has taken place.
Our introductory courses usually last for one day, with follow-up
courses available at a later date.

86

SECOND LEVEL
SET O
CANDIDATES

                Courses
Advanced ~~Training~~   —   bold and underline

    A   C

Our Advanced Courses are designed for users who are already comfortable with producing simple documents or artwork, and who now wish to explore the full potential of the software. Scheduled courses exist for the most commonly-used software packages. However, for other products, advanced training will be tailored to the client's specific needs. After a course of advanced training, you should be able to produce documentation of a highly professional standard.

                                              INSERT AT

Continuation Courses   - bold   (A)

These Courses are designed primarily for clients who have already attended an Introductory Course and who wish to progress to the more advanced features of the software. A pre-course checklist is provided so that delegates can select the aspects which will be of most value to them.

(B)

SECOND LEVEL
SET O
CANDIDATES

On-Site Training — bold and underline

Sometimes it is more appropriate to deliver our training on the customer's own site. This may be a more cost effective option for the organisation and, for the students, learning may be more effective when carried out in a familiar environment.   However, it is vital that an appropriate learning environment is in place for maximum effect.

Tailored Courses   — bold   INSERT AT Ⓑ

If your company wishes to train several members of staff at the same time, we can offer Tailored Courses, whereby the course content is agreed in advance. Practical exercises emulate the real-life situation, so the training becomes more appropriate to your company's needs.

by the employer and course tutor

Workshops   — bold and underline

In addition to our structured courses, we also offer Workshops so that clients can use our software in the presence of one of our trained tutors. Clients can produce work of their own, or work at their own pace through some of our centre-prepared resource packs. To book your place, telephone in advance to check on availability.

Further Information   — bold

If you would like further details, on any of the above courses please contact Rod Lowe on 0171 529 8754 during office hours. Rod will be pleased to send you our latest course schedule.

SECOND LEVEL
SET O
CANDIDATES

ASSIGNMENT 2 - Candidate's Copy

1 Key in the following standard letter with a ragged right margin.

2 Insert merge points at the places shown with an **X** to take the information shown on the next page.

3 Print one copy of this shell letter.

4 Key in the information on the next page as a datafile and print one copy of the file.

5 Merge the datafile with the shell letter and print one copy of each merged letter.

Today's date

JT/

Dear Delegate

Thank you for your completed application form and cheque for Ⓧ. I have pleasure in confirming your place on the forthcoming Ⓧ course.

I enclose with this letter detailed information relating to course content, start and finish times and other matters which you may find useful. However, if you have any further queries, please do not hesitate to contact me.

In the meantime, I look forward to welcoming you to Comlon Computer Training.

Yours sincerely

Jan Tyler
Course Administrator

Enc

SECOND LEVEL
SET O
CANDIDATES

ASSIGNMENT 2 - Candidate's Copy

Mr Surjit Chana
34 Frederick Street
BECKENHAM
BR3 6LP

£293.75
Aldus Pagemaker

Miss Ruth Jefferson
12 Richmond Villas
BRIGHTON
BN5 4DF

£158.62
WordPerfect 5.1

Mrs Eve Wallace
286 Court Road
ORPINGTON
BR6 9AD

£141.00
Excel 5 Advanced

SECOND LEVEL
SET O
CANDIDATES

ASSIGNMENT 3 - Candidate's Copy

Key-in the document below taking care to follow the instructions very carefully. Print out a copy with a justified right hand margin.

bold

COMLON COMPUTER TRAINING

INFORMATION FOR DELEGATES

> CHANGE
> BRANCH TO
> CENTRE
> THROUGHOUT
> THIS ASSIGNMENT

double line spacing
for this paragraph

Comlon Computer Training has been established for ~~more than~~ over 15 years and our highly qualified staff capitalise upon a wealth of training expertise to continually update our practical course material and hands-on training methods. Our primary aim is always to help you acquire a comprehensive knowledge of the software so that you can employ your newly-gained skills in the workplace.

Welcome to Comlon Computer Training. Thank you for enrolling on one of our courses. This information sheet is sent to you with your confirmation letter and we hope that you will spend some time reading about us before you join us for your training session.

SECOND LEVEL
SET O
CANDIDATES

ASSIGNMENT 3 - Candidate's Copy

LOCATION   — bold

We operate from three sites —
our Head Office in Central London and
our satellite branches in Canterbury
and Tonbridge. Each centre is
operational from 9.00 am until
9.00 pm and our welcoming Reception
area (pictured right) is fully manned
at all times. Most of our daytime
courses commence at 9.30 am and
finish at 4.30 pm. Our evening
classes run from 6.30 pm until
8.30 pm. We are also open on

NP Saturday mornings. [Telephone, fax
and photocopying facilities are
available in Reception so that you
can stay in touch with your office if
necessary. Our Receptionists will also
be pleased to take important messages
for you at any time.

Leave a space at
least 3 inches
(75 mm) wide by
3 inches (75 mm)
deep for a
photograph

RESOURCES   - bold

Our clients quite rightly demand and
deserve the best and we have installed
state of the art computing and
printing equipment in all of our
branches. In this way we can deliver
our courses using leading edge
technology. A Resources Centre
(pictured left) on each site ensures
that our clients have access to a
wide range of the latest software
along with the relevant centre-prepared
learning resource packs to allow
effective and continuous learning.

Leave a space at
least 3 inches
(75 mm) wide by
2.5 inches (62 mm)
deep for a
photograph

SECOND LEVEL
SET O
CANDIDATES

ASSIGNMENT 3 - Candidate's Copy

STAFF — bold

Our staff are all experts in their field and are professionally trained to deliver top quality courses to our clients. Several of our tutors regularly travel throughout the world to deliver courses to our overseas clients. Comlon staff have a reputation for being helpful, friendly and informative.

COURSE OUTLINE — bold

When arriving for your course, you will be welcomed to Comlon and registered for your course. You will then be offered refreshments and introduced to your fellow students. We operate with a maximum of 12 students per course, which means that every student gets plenty of attention from the tutor.

Leave a space at least 3 inches (75 mm) wide by 3 inches (75 mm) deep for a photograph

Lunch is provided at a local restaurant (pictured right) and you will be accompanied throughout by your course tutor. This allows for an informal relationship to develop between tutor and student. Coffee and tea are available throughout the day.

HOTLINE SUPPORT — bold

After attending one of our daytime courses, you are eligible for our free hotline technical support which covers any features or techniques taught during your course. Our dedicated team of support engineers is only a telephone call away and, like the rest of Comlon Computer Training, is waiting to help you.

Comlon Computer Training
1997

93

SECOND LEVEL
SET O
CANDIDATES

ASSIGNMENT 4 - PART 1 - Candidate's Copy

Key in the following paragraphs and save them so that they can be used later for boilerplating. Do not key in the numbers unless your system requires them.

1 You should have a basic knowledge of Windows before taking this course.

2 You should have a basic knowledge of DOS before taking this course.

3 An attendance certificate is awarded to all delegates following satisfactory completion of the course.

4 This is a 2-day course, delivered at our Canterbury branch. Numbers are limited to 10 delegates.

5 This is a one-day course, delivered at our Tonbridge branch. Numbers are limited to 12 delegates.

6 Attendance on this course entitles you to 4 hours of free touch typing tuition at the branch of your choice.

7 The aim of the course is to cover all the main features of the package and thereby give delegates the confidence and skill to take their expertise into the workplace.

8 A free follow-up workshop will be offered to all delegates approximately 4 weeks after completion of this course.

SECOND LEVEL
SET O
CANDIDATES

ASSIGNMENT 4 - PART 2 - Candidate's Copy

The shells of 2 documents are given below. Key in the text as 2 separate pages.
The opening paragraph must be displayed as indicated.

Add to each page, in the order shown, the standard paragraphs listed.

COMLON COMPUTER TRAINING

We are pleased to confirm your place on the forthcoming **EXCEL** course. Please
note the following:

(Add paragraphs 7, 1, 4, and 8)

===

COMLON COMPUTER TRAINING

We are pleased to confirm your place on the forthcoming **WORD 6** course. Please
note the following:

(Add paragraphs 7, 5, 3 and 6)

SECOND LEVEL
SET O
CANDIDATES

ASSIGNMENT 5 - PART 1 - Candidate's Copy

Key in the table given below and follow the instructions carefully.

DO NOT USE DITTO MARKS (")

COMLON COMPUTER TRAINING

COURSE FEES

Course Title	Evening Class (20 hours) £	1-day Course (6 hours) £	2-day Course (12 hours) £
Word Perfect 5.1	100.00	75.00	135.00
Word Perfect 5.1 Advanced	"	100.00	–
Word for Windows	120.00	80.00	145.00
Word for Windows Advanced	"	–	150.00
Excel 5	100.00	95.00	180.00
Excel 5 Advanced	"	120.00	–
Aldus Pagemaker	–	–	250.00

Please note that the above fees <u>do not</u> include VAT.

SECOND LEVEL
SET O
CANDIDATES

ASSIGNMENT 5 - PART 2 - Candidate's Copy

Create a form with the headings shown. As the form will be completed by hand,
leave enough space for each of the entries.

COMLON COMPUTER TRAINING

BOOKING FORM

DELEGATE DETAILS

Name . . . .

Address . . . .

. . . .

Postcode . . . . Telephone Number . . . .

Course (s) Required

. . . .

. . . .

. . . .

Signature . . . . Date . . . .

COMPANY DETAILS

Name . . . .

Address . . . .

. . . .

Postcode . . . . Telephone Number . . . .

Contact Name (to whom invoice should be sent) . . . .

This booking form should be accompanied by payment or a
purchase order number. Cheques should be made payable
to Comlon Computer Training Limited.

SECOND LEVEL
SET O
CANDIDATES

ASSIGNMENT 6 - Candidate's Copy

The following document has been left for you to produce. Use your own judgement
with regard to display and print out a copy.

COMLON COMPUTER TRAINING

OPEN ACCESS CENTRE

ComlOn Computer Training ~~are~~ is delighted ~~pleased~~ to announce the
opening of our Open Access Centre for students who wish
to adopt ~~the~~ a truly flexible approach to their computer

NP education. [The Centre, based at our Central London site,
is open from 10 am until 8 pm daily.]

run on Staffed at all times by professional trainers, lthe centre uc
comprises 30 networked personal computers running the
latest business software.

Students may book access to a computer for a one or two
hour period daily and the booking fee includes free use of
our effective learning resource materials.

So, if you want to learn to use the latest software, give
us a call on 0171 529 8754 to book your place!

or merely
surf the Internet

We look forward to welcoming you
to our Open Access Centre soon!

Third Level assignments

**PRACTICAL WORD PROCESSING
THIRD LEVEL**

SPECIMEN ASSIGNMENTS – CANDIDATES

Candidates MUST either write or key-in their names on each printout.

These Assignments are to be used for candidate's final assessment during ....

THIRD LEVEL
SPECIMEN
CANDIDATES

TIME ALLOWANCE

ASSIGNMENT	1	45 minutes
	2	1 hour
	3	1 hour
	4	1 hour
	5	1 hour
	6	45 minutes

TOTAL = 5 hours 30 minutes

THIRD LEVEL
SPECIMEN
CANDIDATES

ASSIGNMENT 1 - Candidate's Copy

1   Key in the following 2-page letter.
2   Number only the second page at the top left.
3   Extract the appropriate information from the information sheet as instructed.
4   Indicate a copy of the letter for Sue Findlay, Promotions Manager.
5   Proofread your work carefully and print 2 copies.
6   Save your work to disk under a meaningful filename (part of this document will be needed for Assignment 3).

STARGAZER TRAVEL PLC — increase font size
Stargazer House
162 Lower Bristol Rd   bold and centre
BATH   BA2 8KM

MK/PD/CONF

← insert name and address of
first prize winner here

Dr ____

STARGAZER HOLIDAY COMPETITION

Further to our telephone conv earlier today, I have great pleasure in confirming that you are the lucky winner of the First Prize in this yr's Stargazer Holiday Comp. You answered all our questions correctly and made up an excellent advertising slogan. In fact, we were so pleased with the slogan that there is a strong possibility that we shall use it in next yr's brochure.

YOUR PRIZE   (As you know,)

Yr prize is a 2-week holiday in China. This all-expense paid trip for 2 people must be taken within the next

THIRD LEVEL
SPECIMEN
CANDIDATES

3 months. Plse let us know yr preferred dates asap so that we can confirm the booking. In addition, you will ~~also~~ receive the sum of £500 to spend as you choose, so you can be sure that your entire family will benefit from yr good fortune!

THE HOLIDAY OF A LIFETIME

We are delighted that you have won our free holiday and we hope that you will take full advantage of all the special

trs   breaks and excursions that we have organised for you. [Your NP itinerary will be as follows:

Day 1	Fly from London Heathrow to Hong Kong
" 2	Hong Kong
Day 3	Fly to Beijing
Days 4 & 5	Beijing including excursion to Great Wall of China
Day 6	Fly to Xian
Day 7	Xian – excursion to the Terracotta Warriors
" 8	Fly to Shanghai
Days 9 & 10	Shanghai
Days 11 ~~& 12~~	Fly to Guilin
Day 12	Guilin and surroundings
13	Return to Beijing
in full 14	Fly to H K and onward flight to UK
Day 15	Arrive London Heathrow

Publicity   INSERT THIS PARAGRAPH AS THE THIRD
                             PARAGRAPH

On Friday next, [insert date] at 1500, we shall be holding a photocall with the local press to announce the competition/results. We should like ~~all our~~ the prizewinners to be present. At this short ceremony, to be held in our Bath office, we will present you with yr prizes. You will also be given a set of executive luggage for yr holiday. Please confirm that you will be able to attend.

THIRD LEVEL
SPECIMEN
CANDIDATES

BUSINESS CLASS ALL THE WAY

You will fly bus class on all flights. You will also be accompanied throughout yr trip by a bilingual guide who will attend to your every need.

We are confident that you will have a wonderful time!

Congratulations on yr success!

Yrs sncly

Mark Kennedy
Managing Director

Once you have confirmed your travel/dates, we will provide you with a more detailed itinerary.

THIRD LEVEL
SPECIMEN
CANDIDATES

ASSIGNMENT 1 - INFORMATION SHEET

STARGAZER TRAVEL PLC

HOLIDAY COMPETITION RESULTS

FIRST PRIZE   2 weeks in China for 2 people
                               £500 spending money
                               Set of luggage

                               WINNER

                               Angela Betts (Mrs)
                               12 Mountjoy Crescent
                               CHIPPENHAM
                               SN8 4RA

                               Tel: 342987

SECOND PRIZE   5 days in Disneyland Paris for 4 people
                               £250 spending money
                               Set of luggage

                               WINNER

                               Jim McCarten
                               34 Belsize Villas
                               BATH
                               BA3 3GD

                               Tel: 276109

THIRD PRIZE   Weekend in Amsterdam for 2 people
                               Set of luggage

                               WINNER

                               Rita Grant (Miss)
                               Flat 2 Copthorne Court
                               CORSHAM
                               SN12 7KM

                               Tel: 345168

THIRD LEVEL
SPECIMEN
CANDIDATES

ASSIGNMENT 2 - Candidate's Copy

1   Key in the table below, following handwritten instructions.
2   Proofread your work carefully and save to disk.
3   Print a copy on A4 landscape.

(title: bold, underline + increased font size)

HOLIDAY INFORMATION - MALAYSIA

HOTEL – *italic*

TOWN	HOTEL	LOCATION	FACILITIES – *italic*					
			TOTAL ROOMS	DINING	POOL	AIR-COND	TV	DIRECT DIAL PHONE
KOTA BAHARU	Perdana	Town Centre	178	3 rests*	Yes	Yes	Yes	Yes
KUANTAN	Cherating	Outskirts of town	125	1 rest	Yes	Yes	"	No
KUCHING	Hilton	Overlooking river	296	3 rests	Yes	Yes	"	Yes
MALACCA	Hotel Suraya	Overlooking beach	210	2 rests	Yes	Yes	"	Yes
SANDAKAN	Renaissance	5 mins from centre	210	1 rest	No	Yes No	"	No
SARAWAK	Danai Beach	On beach	100	2 rests	No	Yes	"	Yes

FLIGHT INFORMATION – *italic*

AIRLINE	AIRCRAFT	UK AIRPORT	DEPARTURE DETAILS – *italic*		
			DEPARTURE DAY	RETURN DAY	NOTES
British Airways	Boeing 747	Heathrow	Daily – Flight No BA 361	Daily – Flight No BA 362	One-stop service
Malaysian Air	Boeing 757	Gatwick	Daily – Flight MA 407	Daily – Flight MA 408	Daylight flight
Southern Air	Boeing 747	Manchester	Mon, Tue, Thur, Fri, Sat	Tue, Wed, Fri, Sat, Sun	–

* expand word (restaurant/restaurants)

(handwritten: RULE AS SHOWN)

(handwritten: Shade these rows and embolden the titles)

THIRD LEVEL
SPECIMEN
CANDIDATES

ASSIGNMENT 3 - Candidate's Copy

1   Recall the following document to your screen, stored as [   ] and edit as shown.
2   Repaginate sensibly and number each page at the bottom centre. Page numbers
     should commence at 15.
3   Insert a header KEY NOTES at the top right of each page.
4   Insert footnotes as appropriate.
5   Proofread your work carefully and save to disk.
6   Print a copy on A4 portrait.

CHINA   — *bold and underline*

① General Information   — *caps*

Population:	1 billion
Area:	3,695,500 square miles
Currency:	Chinese Yuan
	US $ readily accepted
Distance from UK:	5053 miles
Flying time:	*10 hours*
GMT:	*+8 hours*

ARRANGE ITEMS IN ORDER INDICATED BUT DO NOT NUMBER

② CLIMATE

The climate *in China* varies considerably from place to place. As a guide the temperature in Beijing alone ranges from 2°C in Jan to over 31°C in July and Aug.

④ FLIGHTS

International flights in and out of Beijing are *seldom* ~~never~~ affected by delay. Internal flights can ~~however~~ be problematic, with unscheduled re-routing[1] and cancellation.

---

[1] *The substitution of a flight with a ground alternative may be necessary.*

106

THIRD LEVEL
SPECIMEN
CANDIDATES

③ HEALTH REQUIREMENTS

The following vaccinations are recommended for all parts of China:

Polio
Typhoid
Yellow fever
Malaria
Hepatitis A

indent this text 38 mm (1.5 inches) from left margin

Travellers must ensure that they are in possession of the relevant vaccination certificates before undertaking their travel.

⑦ VISA INFORMATION

A full 10-year passport with at least 6 months' validity from the date of departure is ~~need~~ required. A visa is also required[2].

A Visa Application Form and guidelines must be sent to all travellers on confirmation of their booking.

It is the responsibility of the traveller to ensure that all necessary documentation is acquired prior to departure.

⑤ MAIN SITES

We anticipate that most visitors will wish to visit four ~~main~~ major sites:

BEIJING   Situated in the north, Beijing is a bustling city with several deluxe hotels. Visit the Forbidden City, the Summer Palace and the Ming Tombs. Just a short drive from Beijing is the Great Wall of China.

---

[2] For travellers planning to visit China after Hong Kong, a visa must be acquired in the UK

THIRD LEVEL
SPECIMEN
CANDIDATES

GUILIN — Located in the southern agricultural region, Guilin is justly famous for its spectacular landscapes of paddy fields and mountains. The Li River offers cruises to visitors.

tls

SHANGHAI — Shanghai, one of China's greatest cities, is a bustling port offering exciting nightlife to tourists. The Grand Canal runs through the city. Visit the Bund, a busy waterfront boulevard, the Children's Palace and the Jade Buddha Temple.

XIAN — Xian is the site of the burial tomb of the Terracotta Warriors which were unearthed in the 1970s. Local excursions to hot springs and a Neolithic settlement are available from this location.

⑥ ITINERARIES

It is expected that /~~visitors~~ travellers to China will be accompanied throughout their visit by a bilingual guide and will undertake a multi-centre holiday. A typical itinerary wd be as follows:

(INSERT ITINERARY FROM ASSIGNMENT 1)

As the ~~num~~ number of travellers increases, so will the variety of itinerary be widened.

⑧ BEST BUYS

There are many small outdoor markets in China in which items such as jade, antique ceramics, silk garments and wood, stone and bamboo carvings can be found. It is customary to

NP
bargain. [In the larger department stores, prices are fixed.

Stargazer Travel PLC
[Date]

THIRD LEVEL
SPECIMEN
CANDIDATES

ASSIGNMENT 4 - Candidate's Copy

1   Key in the text below, using a consistent typeface, to produce a two-column
     newsletter.
2   Use a fully-justified right margin.
3   Proofread your work and save to disk.
4   Print out a copy on A4 portrait.

use 16 point for both lines

Stargazer   News — _underline_

Keeping you in touch with reality

use shading and a border

WELCOME

Welcome to all our readers. This is only the second issue of Stargazer News but we have been delighted by the response to our first issue. Please keep us informed of current news from your branch. Send your information to Sally Webb at Head Office.

HOLIDAY COMPETITION

Mark Kennedy recently announced the winners of this year's competition. The first prize winner is Mrs Angela Betts of Chippenham. She'll be taking her husband Raymond with her when they travel to China for a 2-week holiday later this year.

New Key Notes

You should soon be in receipt of a new set of Key Notes. The topic is China. Please make sure that you ~~study~~ _read_ them carefully and ~~keep~~ _retain_ them for future reference. We are hoping to expand our multi-centre holidays in China over the coming months. We'll keep you informed. Special offers are in the pipeline.

THIRD LEVEL
SPECIMEN
CANDIDATES

OPEN ALL HOURS

With effect from next week, Stargazer will be accessible on the Internet. Our website will give details of holiday destinations as well as examples of special travel offers. Let our customers know that they can contact us on www.stars.co.uk!

STAFF DEVELOPMENT

Any ~~member of~~ staff who wishes to

undertake training in a non-European

language should contact Luisa de Valera

at Head Office who will be happy to

advise you.

space→ **CHEAPER TRAVEL INSURANCE**
The introduction of our new annual travel insurance ~~insurance~~ policy has proved to be very popular among our regular customers. It is by far the cheapest way to insure a family of four who typically take just two holidays a year. ~~Prices~~ *rates* start at only £58.

New
~~Updated~~ publicity leaflets are currently being prepared and will be delivered to your branches ~~shortly.~~ very soon.

ANNUAL STAFF GET-TOGETHER

This year it has been decided to organise a weekend in London instead of the usual Staff Dinner and Dance.
The weekend will take place in *late* October and will include a staff

dinner and a trip to a West End Show. Partners are welcome ~~to~~

~~join us~~. The weekend will be free of charge to employees with a minimal charge to guests. Let Rob Atkins know if you wish to join us.

CONGRATULATIONS

Anna Jones of our Cardiff branch recently gave birth to twins. Many congratulations, Anna! We're looking forward to seeing you soon.

THIRD LEVEL
SPECIMEN
CANDIDATES

ASSIGNMENT 5 - Candidate's Copy

1   Key in the following document expanding abbreviations.
2   Use a justified right hand margin.
3   Number the second page at the bottom centre.
4   Follow any other instructions which appear within the document.
5   Proofread carefully and save your work to disk.
6   Print out a copy on A4 portrait.

~~DRAFT~~

STARGAZER TRAVEL PLC   – bold

                    THE
MINUTES OF/MEETING of the Committee held on .....✓......... at 1430 in the ~~Board~~ Conference Room.

[insert today's date]

PRESENT   Mark Kennedy (Chairman)
                 Judy Grover (Secretary)
                 Sue Findlay
                 Robert Williams
                 ~~Sally Knights~~ Des Marchant
                 ~~Sanjit Patel~~ Luisa de Valera

1   APOLOGIES FOR ABSENCE
        There were no apologies for absence.
        ~~Apologies were recieved from Ruth Thompson.~~

2   MINUTES OF LAST MEETING

        The Minutes of the last meeting were agreed and signed.

3   MATTERS ARISING

                                                    very pleased
3.1   Mark Kennedy reported that ~~the~~ shareholders were ~~delighted~~ with ~~the company's~~
        recent performance and that plans for further expansion were a distinct possibility.
        He will report again following his meeting with the Board next wk.

4   PRIZE COMPETITION

        Sue Findlay reported that the winner of the Stargazer Holiday Competition was ~~won~~
        ~~by~~ Mrs Angela Betts of Chippenham. Mrs Betts and ~~a partner~~ her husband will travel to China for
        a 2-week break. A photocall was arranged with the local press.

        Action: Sue Findlay

        3.2   Des Marchant confirmed that
                Holidays Incorporated had gone
                into liquidation.

THIRD LEVEL
SPECIMEN
CANDIDATES

5 NEW DESTINATIONS

5.1 SOUTH AMERICA

~~5.1~~ *trs* Luisa de Valera commented that, owing to public demand for more exotic holidays, Chile and Peru were being investigated as possible new *holiday* destinations.

Hotels were generally of good quality and able to offer ~~excellent~~ *lucrative* discounts. Two-centre holidays were considered to be more attractive than tours *or single-centre holidays.*

Action: Luisa de Valera

5.2 JAPAN

Sue Findlay reported that last year more than 30 clients travelled to Japan for recreational purposes.

Following discussion ~~it was~~ *the Committee* felt that exclusive package holidays to Japan might have limited success. It was agreed to contact the travellers and request their comments.

Action: Sue Findlay

~~8~~ 7 ANY OTHER BUSINESS

There was no other business.

8 DATE AND TIME OF NEXT MEETING

Wednesday (*insert date of 2nd Wed of next month*) at 1430.

Chairman .... Date ....

---

insert this as point number 6

6 FOREIGN LANGUAGE TRAINING

uc

It was felt that foreign language skills amongst Head office ~~staff~~ staff were sadly lacking. Faxes and telephone messages from overseas were often unintelligible *owing* ~~due~~ to ~~basic~~ lack of linguistic knowledge. Mark Kennedy suggested that basic foreign lang training shd be made available to all staff as Staff Development. Luisa de Valera agreed to contact colleagues in the education sector.

Action: Luisa de Valera

THIRD LEVEL
SPECIMEN
CANDIDATES

ASSIGNMENT 6 - Candidate's Copy

1   Key in the text below, following instructions.
2   Use a fully justified right margin.
3   Size and position the graphic as instructed.
4   Centre the text vertically on the page.
5   Proof-read carefully and print out a copy of your work.

STARGAZER TRAVEL INSURANCE

— MAKE SURE YOU'RE FULLY COVERED!   } bold and centre

When arranging a holiday for yourself and yr family, we know that you don't like to cut costs. You quite naturally want to treat your loved ones to a ~~tasty~~ memorable experience ... and so a considerable length of time is spent planning your ~~holiday.~~ trip.

insert a suitable graphic here measuring 50mm (2 inches) across by 50 mm (2 inches) deep. Use a double border to surround the graphic.

run on (But what about travel insurance? How much time do you spend on that? Our survey shows that the average ~~person~~ traveller spends no more than 5 minutes organising insurance. So, is it any surprise that when claims are made, the results are often disappointing?

Think about an alternative ...   — bold
(at Stargazer Travel)

We would like to tell you about our Annual Travel Insurance. It's an annual policy designed for ~~all~~ families and individuals who travel abroad more than once a year. It is available for everyone under ~~the age~~ 70 years of age. Premiums can be paid monthly or annually by direct debit. The policy covers both business & holiday travel and there is no ~~restriction~~ limit to the number of trips that can be taken during the one-year period.

uc

The only restriction ~~refers~~ relates to Winter sports cover — one trip of up to 21 days' duration is permissible.

How much does it cost?　　— bold

The Stargazer Annual Travel Insurance Policy costs only £60 per adult per year. Let's imagine a family of four who travel abroad twice a year (2 weeks in the Summer and a 1-week skiing holiday in the Winter).

Children between the ages of 2 and 15 years cost £26 each.

Cost of premium = £60 + £60 + £26 + £26 = £172
Length of holiday = 21 days

Cost of cover = £172 ÷ 21 = £8.19 per day　　　— bold

We think that's a small prize to pay for the satisfaction of knowing that your/whole family is covered against ~~illness~~, accident, illness, loss of baggage, cancellation + personal liability.

CONTACT YOUR STARGAZER TRAVEL AGENT NOW FOR AN APPLICATION FORM

What's more, the Winter Sports cover includes loss, theft or damage to equipment, cover against piste closure or avalanche and inability to ski due to illness or injury.

10

Tutor copies

First Level tutor copy

**EXAMINATIONS
BOARD**

**PRACTICAL WORD PROCESSING
FIRST LEVEL**

SET 19 – TUTORS

Candidates MUST either write or key-in their names on each printout.

These Assignments are to be used for candidate's final assessment during 1997

FIRST LEVEL
SET 19
TUTORS

TIME ALLOWANCE

ASSIGNMENT 1   30 minutes

            2   30 minutes

            3   30 minutes

            4   30 minutes

            5   30 minutes

            6   30 minutes

TOTAL = 3 hours

FIRST LEVEL
SET 19
TUTORS

ASSIGNMENT 1 - Marking Guide

SERVICES FOR THOSE WHO ARE SICK OR ELDERLY

The care services through which elderly or sick people can obtain help meet an important need. That is why it is so necessary to provide a complete directory of home care services and nursing homes where people can stay. It can provide information on the many different kinds of places available and will also offer useful advice on what to consider before any decision is made.

It is important that anyone thinking about moving into such a place should have the best possible information in order to choose wisely. Those having to make a choice on behalf of relatives have a more difficult task and must seek other advice as well.

Candidate's Name

FIRST LEVEL
SET 19
TUTORS

ASSIGNMENT 2 – Marking Guide

THE RELATIVES ASSOCIATION
200 Chiswell Street
LONDON
EC2Y 3BU

BR/

Today's date

Mrs R Curtis
125 Windmill Road
CHESHUNT
Herts
EN7 4SP

Dear Mrs Curtis

THE RELATIVES ASSOCIATION

Thank you for your enquiry regarding our Association. Further details about our services are provided in the attached leaflet.

The Association is now a registered charity and is given a grant from the Department of Health. Fund raising is still necessary however.

The Relatives Association tries to achieve the best possible standards of care both at home and in nursing homes. It was founded in 1992 by a group of people who experienced similar problems when an elderly relative needed to be cared for at home or moved into a nursing home.

Sometimes the need for a relative to be cared for at home or moved into a home has been sudden. Quite often a decision has been reached after a long period of care by a husband, wife, son or daughter. In any event the decision is often very difficult.

The Relatives Association is there to help sort out any aspects of concern. Our officers may be called upon when trouble strikes.

Yours sincerely

Belinda Reeves
Association Secretary

Enc

FIRST LEVEL
SET 19
TUTORS

ASSIGNMENT 3 - Marking Guide

COMLON HOMECARE

A HELPING HAND

COMLON HOMECARE provides a range of
flexible, individual care services as required,
24 hours a day,
all year round.

This enables people of any age or disability
to live as normal a life as possible
in the comfort and security of their own homes.

To fulfil the needs of clients,
COMLON HOMECARE provides:

* 1 to 24 hour cover

* Personal and social care

* Practical support

* Other related home care services

* Community alarm and monitoring service

For further details or a visit from one of our officers
contact your local **COMLON HOMECARE** branch
01845 284401

FIRST LEVEL
SET 19
TUTORS

ASSIGNMENT 4 - Marking Guide

MEMORANDUM

To   P Walter, Senior Officer

From   Belinda Reeves, Association Secretary

Ref   BR/

Date   Today's date

DIFFERENT TYPES OF CARE HOMES

In giving help and advice to our clients your staff must first investigate other sources of help. These will include Local Authorities and private nursing organisations. In addition there are voluntary organisations and charitable trusts. All can provide care by skilled staff 24 hours a day either in a home or by home nursing care.

Ensure that they inform clients that a residential care home is not a nursing home. People who need nursing care will need the additional support of the District Nursing Service. In their investigations remind your staff that when people go into a home it should feel just like going into their own homes. It should provide a homely environment and meet the needs of the individual. Also it should promote dignity, independence and continued personal development.

Above all the purpose of such care is to enable people to live enjoyable, independent and fulfilled lives as far as possible.

FIRST LEVEL
SET 19
TUTORS

ASSIGNMENT 5 - Marking Guide

MOVING INTO A CARE HOME

If you are thinking it is time to move to a Care Home you are faced with some very important decisions and choices. You will need information about the choices available and guidance about the questions you may wish to ask before reaching a decision.

It would be useful to use the following as a **CHECKLIST** to help you make your decision.

CONDITIONS

Can you retain your room if away and is it possible to have a short stay or trial period before signing an agreement? Will you be given a statement of terms and conditions on admission?

FEES

How much are the fees and what do the fees include? Do they include services and consumables such as toiletries? Under what circumstances will fees alter eg annually, or according to care needs?

ACCOMMODATION

Are there communal sitting rooms with/without TV and video? Will you have to share a bedroom or bathroom and if so with how many other residents? Is there adequate wheelchair access indoors and outdoors; are handrails provided in hallways and corridors?

TRANSPORT

Is the home easy to get to for relatives and friends and how close is it to community facilities? Does the home provide its own transport and do residents pay extra for this?

CATERING

Is there a choice of menu at each meal and are special requirements catered for ie vegetarians, diabetics?

FIRST LEVEL
SET 19
TUTORS
ASSIGNMENT 6 - Marking Guide

RELATIVES ASSOCIATION MEETING

Minutes of the meeting held on (today's date) at 200 Chiswell Street, London, EC2Y 3BU at 1400.

PRESENT   Belinda Reeves (Chairperson)
                    Paula Walter
                    Rita Jones
                    Hilary Edwards

APOLOGIES FOR ABSENCE

No apologies for absence were received.

MINUTES OF PREVIOUS MEETING

The minutes of the last meeting were approved and signed.

MATTERS ARISING

There were no matters arising.

RECRUITING OF OFFICERS

Paula Walter reported that the recruitment of officers was progressing well. She was looking for suitable applicants very experienced in the field of care services. Interviews start next week.

TRAINING COURSES

Officers will be invited to attend a training course for letter writing and telephone skills to be held next month. Hilary Edwards will be making the arrangements.

RENEWAL OF CHARITY REGISTRATION

Belinda Reeves reported that the confirmation for renewal had been received and that our Registered Charity No was 1920000. The Association is to receive a grant from the Department of Health.

ANY OTHER BUSINESS

Belinda Reeves stated that the Association was receiving details from more home care establishments. These should be looked into carefully before being offered to clients.

The Association regretted the resignation of Rita Jones who would be moving to Scotland and thanked her for her excellent services.

DATE OF NEXT MEETING

To be advised.

Second Level tutor copy

EXAMINATIONS
BOARD

**PRACTICAL WORD PROCESSING
SECOND LEVEL**

SET O – TUTORS

Candidates MUST either write or key-in their names on each printout.

These Assignments are to be used for candidate's final assessment during 1997

SECOND LEVEL
SET O
TUTORS

TIME ALLOWANCE

ASSIGNMENT	1		1 hour
	2		1 hour
	3		1 hour
	4	Part 1	30 minutes
		Part 2	30 minutes
	5	Part 1	30 minutes
		Part 2	30 minutes
	6		30 minutes

TOTAL = 5 hours 30 minutes

SECOND LEVEL
SET O
TUTORS
ASSIGNMENT 1 - Marking Guide

SHORT COURSES

COMLON COMPUTER TRAINING

COURSE INFORMATION

Comlon Computer Training offers a wide range of courses for students of all ages and abilities. Whether you are a complete beginner, or already have extensive computing skills, we offer courses at all levels to suit your particular needs. Our courses run throughout the year too, so you, the client, can choose the timing of your training to suit your individual needs. We also have three sites - our Head Office in Central London, and two satellite branches in Canterbury and Tonbridge.

Introductory Courses

These courses are designed for users with little or no experience of the software package. No previous knowledge is assumed, but it is helpful to have basic keyboarding skills. All of the basic functions of the software package are covered, and consolidation exercises ensure that learning has taken place. Our introductory courses usually last for one day, with follow-up courses available at a later date.

Continuation Courses

These courses are designed primarily for clients who have already attended an Introductory Course and who wish to progress to the more advanced features of the software. A pre-course checklist is provided so that delegates can select the aspects which will be of most value to them.

SECOND LEVEL
SET O
TUTORS

Advanced Courses

Our Advanced Courses are designed for users who are already comfortable with producing simple documents or artwork, and who now wish to explore the full potential of the software. Scheduled courses exist for the most commonly-used software packages. However, for other products, advanced training will be tailored to the client's specific needs. After a course of advanced training, you should be able to produce documentation of a highly professional standard.

Tailored Courses

If your company wishes to train several members of staff at the same time, we can offer Tailored Courses, whereby the course content is agreed by the employer and course tutor in advance. Practical exercises emulate the real-life situation, so the training becomes more appropriate to your company's needs.

On-Site Training

Sometimes it is more appropriate to deliver our training on the customer's own site. This may be a more cost effective option for the organisation and, for the students, learning may be more effective when carried out in a familiar environment. However, it is vital that an appropriate learning environment is in place for maximum effect.

SECOND LEVEL
SET O
TUTORS

SHORT COURSES

Workshops

In addition to our structured courses, we also offer Workshops so that clients can use our software in the presence of one of our trained tutors. Clients can produce work of their own, or work at their own pace through some of our centre-prepared resource packs. To book your place, telephone in advance to check on availability.

Further Information

If you would like further details on any of the above courses, please contact Rod Lowe on 0171 529 8754 during office hours. Rod will be pleased to send you our latest course schedule.

SECOND LEVEL
SET O
TUTORS

ASSIGNMENT 2 - Marking Guide

JT/

Today's date

(Name)
(Address 1)
(Address 2)
(Address 3)

Dear Delegate

Thank you for your completed application form and cheque for (amount). I have pleasure in confirming your place on the forthcoming (course title) course.

I enclose with this letter detailed information relating to course content, start and finish times and other matters which you may find useful. However, if you have any further queries, please do not hesitate to contact me.

In the meantime, I look forward to welcoming you to Comlon Computer Training.

Yours sincerely

Jan Tyler
Course Administrator

Enc

SECOND LEVEL
SET O
TUTORS

ASSIGNMENT 2 - Marking Guide

Mr Surjit Chana
34 Frederick Street
BECKENHAM
BR3 6LP

£293.75
Aldus Pagemaker

Miss Ruth Jefferson
12 Richmond Villas
BRIGHTON
BN5 4DF

£158.62
WordPerfect 5.1

Mrs Eve Wallace
286 Court Road
ORPINGTON
BR6 9AD

£141.00
Excel 5 Advanced

SECOND LEVEL
SET O
TUTORS
ASSIGNMENT 2 - Marking Guide

JT/

Today's date

Mr Surjit Chana
34 Frederick Street
BECKENHAM
BR3 6LP

Dear Delegate

Thank you for your completed application form and cheque for £293.75. I have pleasure in confirming your place on the forthcoming Aldus Pagemaker course.

I enclose with this letter detailed information relating to course content, start and finish times and other matters which you may find useful. However, if you have any further queries, please do not hesitate to contact me.

In the meantime, I look forward to welcoming you to Comlon Computer Training.

Yours sincerely

Jan Tyler
Course Administrator

Enc

SECOND LEVEL
SET O
TUTORS
ASSIGNMENT 2 - Marking Guide

JT/

Today's date

Miss Ruth Jefferson
12 Richmond Villas
BRIGHTON
BN5 4DF

Dear Delegate

Thank you for your completed application form and cheque for £158.62. I have pleasure in confirming your place on the forthcoming WordPerfect 5.1 course.

I enclose with this letter detailed information relating to course content, start and finish times and other matters which you may find useful. However, if you have any further queries, please do not hesitate to contact me.

In the meantime, I look forward to welcoming you to Comlon Computer Training.

Yours sincerely

Jan Tyler
Course Administrator

Enc

SECOND LEVEL
SET O
TUTORS
ASSIGNMENT 2 - Marking Guide

JT/

Today's date

Mrs Eve Wallace
286 Court Road
ORPINGTON
BR6 9AD

Dear Delegate

Thank you for your completed application form and cheque for £141.00. I have pleasure in confirming your place on the forthcoming Excel 5 Advanced course.

I enclose with this letter detailed information relating to course content, start and finish times and other matters which you may find useful. However, if you have any further queries, please do not hesitate to contact me.

In the meantime, I look forward to welcoming you to Comlon Computer Training.

Yours sincerely

Jan Tyler
Course Administrator

Enc

SECOND LEVEL
SET O
TUTORS

ASSIGNMENT 3 - Marking Guide

COMLON COMPUTER TRAINING

INFORMATION FOR DELEGATES

Welcome to Comlon Computer Training. Thank you for enrolling on one of our courses. This information sheet is sent to you with your confirmation letter and we hope that you will spend some time reading about us before you join us for your training session.

Comlon Computer Training has been established for over 15 years and our highly qualified staff capitalise upon a wealth of training expertise to continually update our hands-on training methods and practical course material. Our primary aim is always to help you acquire a comprehensive knowledge of the software so that you can employ your newly-gained skills in the workplace.

LOCATION

We operate from three sites - our Head Office in Central London and our satellite centres in Canterbury and Tonbridge. Each centre is operational from 9.00 am until 9.00 pm and our welcoming Reception area (pictured right) is fully manned at all times. Most of our daytime courses commence at 9.30 am and finish at 4.30 pm. Our evening classes run from 6.30 pm until 8.30 pm. We are also open on Saturday mornings.

Telephone, fax and photocopying facilities are available in Reception so that you can stay in touch with your office if necessary. Our Receptionists will also be pleased to take important messages for you at any time.

SECOND LEVEL
SET O
TUTORS

RESOURCES

Our clients quite rightly demand and deserve the best and we have installed state of the art computing and printing equipment in all of our centres. In this way we can deliver our courses using leading edge technology. A Resources Centre (pictured left) on each site ensures that our clients have access to a wide range of the latest software along with the relevant centre-prepared learning resource packs to allow effective and continuous learning.

STAFF

Our staff are all experts in their field and are professionally trained to deliver top quality courses to our clients. Several of our tutors regularly travel throughout the world to deliver courses to our overseas clients. Comlon staff have a reputation for being helpful, friendly and informative.

COURSE OUTLINE

When arriving for your course, you will be welcomed to Comlon and registered for your course. You will then be offered refreshments and introduced to your fellow students. We operate with a maximum of 12 students per course, which means that every student gets plenty of attention from the tutor.

Lunch is provided at a local restaurant (pictured right) and you will be accompanied throughout by your course tutor. This allows for an informal relationship to develop between tutor and student. Coffee and tea are available throughout the day.

HOTLINE SUPPORT

After attending one of our daytime courses, you are eligible for our free hotline technical support which covers any features or techniques taught during your course. Our dedicated team of support engineers is only a telephone call away and, like the rest of Comlon Computer Training, is waiting to help you.

Comlon Computer Training
1997

SECOND LEVEL
SET O
TUTORS

ASSIGNMENT 4 - PART 1 - Marking Guide

1 You should have a basic knowledge of Windows before taking this course.

2 You should have a basic knowledge of DOS before taking this course.

3 An attendance certificate is awarded to all delegates following satisfactory completion of the course.

4 This is a 2-day course, delivered at our Canterbury branch. Numbers are limited to 10 delegates.

5 This is a one-day course, delivered at our Tonbridge branch. Numbers are limited to 12 delegates.

6 Attendance on this course entitles you to 4 hours of free touch typing tuition at the branch of your choice.

7 The aim of the course is to cover all the main features of the package and thereby give delegates the confidence and skill to take their expertise into the workplace.

8 A free follow-up workshop will be offered to all delegates approximately 4 weeks after completion of this course.

SECOND LEVEL
SET O
TUTORS

ASSIGNMENT 4 - PART 2 - Marking Guide

COMLON COMPUTER TRAINING

We are pleased to confirm your place on the forthcoming **EXCEL** course. Please note the following:

The aim of the course is to cover all the main features of the package and thereby give delegates the confidence and skill to take their expertise into the workplace.

You should have a basic knowledge of Windows before taking this course.

This is a 2-day course, delivered at our Canterbury branch. Numbers are limited to 10 delegates.

A free follow-up workshop will be offered to all delegates approximately 4 weeks after completion of this course.

SECOND LEVEL
SET O
TUTORS
ASSIGNMENT 4 - PART 2 - Marking Guide

COMLON COMPUTER TRAINING

We are pleased to confirm your place on the forthcoming **WORD 6** course. Please note the following:

The aim of the course is to cover all the main features of the package and thereby give delegates the confidence and skill to take their expertise into the workplace.

This is a one-day course, delivered at our Tonbridge branch. Numbers are limited to 12 delegates.

An attendance certificate is awarded to all delegates following satisfactory completion of the course.

Attendance on this course entitles you to 4 hours of free touch typing tuition at the branch of your choice.

SECOND LEVEL
SET O
TUTORS

ASSIGNMENT 5 - **PART 1** - Marking Guide

COMLON COMPUTER TRAINING

COURSE FEES

Course Title	1-day Course (6 hours) £	2-day Course (12 hours) £	Evening Class (20 hours) £
WordPerfect 5.1	75.00	135.00	100.00
WordPerfect 5.1 Advanced	100.00	—	100.00
Word for Windows	80.00	145.00	120.00
Word for Windows Advanced	—	150.00	120.00
Excel 5	95.00	180.00	100.00
Excel 5 Advanced	120.00	—	100.00
Aldus Pagemaker	—	250.00	—

Please note that the above fees do not include VAT.

SECOND LEVEL
SET O
TUTORS

ASSIGNMENT 5 - PART 2 - Marking Guide

COMLON COMPUTER TRAINING

BOOKING FORM

DELEGATE DETAILS

Name ....

Address ....

....

Postcode .... Telephone Number ....

Course(s) Required

....

....

....

Signature .... Date ....

COMPANY DETAILS

Name ....

Address ....

....

Postcode .... Telephone Number ....

Contact Name (to whom invoice should be sent) ....

This booking form should be accompanied by payment or a purchase order number.
Cheques should be made payable to Comlon Computer Training Limited.

SECOND LEVEL
SET O
TUTORS

ASSIGNMENT 6 - Marking Guide

COMLON COMPUTER TRAINING

OPEN ACCESS CENTRE

Comlon Computer Training is delighted to announce the opening of our Open Access Centre for students who wish to adopt a truly flexible approach to their computer education.

The Centre, based at our Central London site, is open from 10 am until 8 pm daily. Staffed at all times by professional trainers, the Centre comprises 30 networked personal computers running the latest business software.

Students may book access to a computer for a one or two hour period daily and the booking fee includes free use of our effective learning resource materials.

So, if you want to learn to use the latest software or merely surf the Internet, give us a call on 0171 529 8754 to book your place!

**We look forward to welcoming you
to our Open Access Centre soon!**

Third Level tutor copy

**EXAMINATIONS
BOARD**

**PRACTICAL WORD PROCESSING
THIRD LEVEL**

SPECIAL ASSIGNMENTS – TUTORS

Candidates MUST either write or key-in their names on each printout.

These Assignments are to be used for candidate's final assessment during ....

THIRD LEVEL
SPECIMEN
TUTORS

TIME ALLOWANCE FOR CANDIDATES

ASSIGNMENT	1	45 minutes
	2	1 hour
	3	1 hour
	4	1 hour
	5	1 hour
	6	45 minutes

TOTAL = 5 hours 30 minutes

THIRD LEVEL
SPECIMEN
TUTORS

THIRD LEVEL
SPECIMEN
TUTORS

ASSIGNMENT 1 - Marking Guide

STARGAZER TRAVEL PLC

**Stargazer House
162 Lower Bristol Road
BATH BA2 8KM**

MK/PD/CONF

Date

Mrs Angela Betts
12 Mountjoy Crescent
CHIPPENHAM
SN8 4RA

Dear Mrs Betts

STARGAZER HOLIDAY COMPETITION

Further to our telephone conversation earlier today, I have great pleasure in confirming that
you are the lucky winner of the First Prize in this year's Stargazer Holiday Competition. You
answered all our questions correctly and made up an excellent advertising slogan. In fact,
we were so pleased with the slogan that there is a strong possibility that we shall use it in
next year's brochure.

YOUR PRIZE

As you know, your prize is a 2-week holiday in China. This all-expense paid trip for 2 people
must be taken within the next 3 months. Please let us know your preferred dates as soon
as possible so that we can confirm the booking. In addition, you will receive the sum of
£500 to spend as you choose, so you can be sure that your entire family will benefit from
your good fortune!

PUBLICITY

On Friday next, [date] at 1500, we shall be holding a photocall with the local press to
announce the competition results. We should like the prizewinners to be present. At this
short ceremony, to be held in our Bath office, we will present you with your prizes. You will
also be given a set of executive luggage for your holiday. Please confirm that you will be
able to attend.

THIRD LEVEL
SPECIMEN
TUTORS

2

THE HOLIDAY OF A LIFETIME

We are delighted that you have won our free holiday and we hope that you will take full advantage of all the special excursions and treats that we have organised for you.

Your itinerary will be as follows:

Day 1	Fly from London Heathrow to Hong Kong
Day 2	Hong Kong
Day 3	Fly to Beijing
Days 4 and 5	Beijing including excursion to Great Wall of China
Day 6	Fly to Xian
Day 7	Xian - excursion to the Terracotta Warriors
Day 8	Fly to Shanghai
Days 9 and 10	Shanghai
Day 11	Fly to Guilin
Day 12	Guilin and surroundings
Day 13	Return to Beijing
Day 14	Fly to Hong Kong and onward flight to UK
Day 15	Arrive London Heathrow

BUSINESS CLASS ALL THE WAY

Once you have confirmed your travel dates, we will provide you with a more detailed itinerary. You will fly business class on all flights. You will also be accompanied throughout your trip by a bilingual guide who will attend to your every need.

We are confident that you will have a wonderful time!

Congratulations on your success!

Yours sincerely

Mark Kennedy
Managing Director

Copy to Sue Findlay, Promotions Manager

THIRD LEVEL
SPECIMEN
TUTORS

ASSIGNMENT 1 - Marking Guide

STARGAZER TRAVEL PLC

**Stargazer House
162 Lower Bristol Road
BATH BA2 8KM**

MK/PD/CONF

Date

Mrs Angela Betts
12 Mountjoy Crescent
CHIPPENHAM
SN8 4RA

Dear Mrs Betts

STARGAZER HOLIDAY COMPETITION

Further to our telephone conversation earlier today, I have great pleasure in confirming that you are the lucky winner of the First Prize in this year's Stargazer Holiday Competition. You answered all our questions correctly and made up an excellent advertising slogan. In fact, we were so pleased with the slogan that there is a strong possibility that we shall use it in next year's brochure.

YOUR PRIZE

As you know, your prize is a 2-week holiday in China. This all-expense paid trip for 2 people must be taken within the next 3 months. Please let us know your preferred dates as soon as possible so that we can confirm the booking. In addition, you will receive the sum of £500 to spend as you choose, so you can be sure that your entire family will benefit from your good fortune!

PUBLICITY

On Friday next, [date] at 1500, we shall be holding a photocall with the local press to announce the competition results. We should like the prizewinners to be present. At this short ceremony, to be held in our Bath office, we will present you with your prizes. You will also be given a set of executive luggage for your holiday. Please confirm that you will be able to attend.

THIRD LEVEL
SPECIMEN
TUTORS

2

THE HOLIDAY OF A LIFETIME

We are delighted that you have won our free holiday and we hope that you will take full advantage of all the special excursions and treats that we have organised for you.

Your itinerary will be as follows:

Day 1	Fly from London Heathrow to Hong Kong
Day 2	Hong Kong
Day 3	Fly to Beijing
Days 4 and 5	Beijing including excursion to Great Wall of China
Day 6	Fly to Xian
Day 7	Xian - excursion to the Terracotta Warriors
Day 8	Fly to Shanghai
Days 9 and 10	Shanghai
Day 11	Fly to Guilin
Day 12	Guilin and surroundings
Day 13	Return to Beijing
Day 14	Fly to Hong Kong and onward flight to UK
Day 15	Arrive London Heathrow

BUSINESS CLASS ALL THE WAY

Once you have confirmed your travel dates, we will provide you with a more detailed itinerary. You will fly business class on all flights. You will also be accompanied throughout your trip by a bilingual guide who will attend to your every need.

We are confident that you will have a wonderful time!

Congratulations on your success!

Yours sincerely

Mark Kennedy
Managing Director

Copy to Sue Findlay, Promotions Manager

ASSIGNMENT 2 - Marking Guide

HOLIDAY INFORMATION – MALAYSIA

HOTEL

TOWN	HOTEL	LOCATION	TOTAL ROOMS	FACILITIES				
				DINING	POOL	AIR-COND	TV	DIRECT DIAL PHONE
KOTA BAHARU	Perdana	Town centre	178	3 restaurants	Yes	Yes	Yes	Yes
KUANTAN	Cherating	Outskirts of town	125	1 restaurant	Yes	Yes	Yes	No
KUCHING	Hilton	Overlooking river	296	3 restaurants	Yes	Yes	Yes	Yes
MALACCA	Hotel Suraya	Overlooking beach	210	2 restaurants	Yes	Yes	Yes	Yes
SANDAKAN	Renaissance	5 mins from centre	100	1 restaurant	No	No	Yes	No
SARAWAK	Damai Beach	On beach	210	2 restaurants	No	Yes	Yes	Yes

FLIGHT INFORMATION

DEPARTURE DETAILS

AIRLINE	AIRCRAFT	UK AIRPORT	DEPARTURE DAY	RETURN DAY	NOTES
British Airways	Boeing 747	Heathrow	Daily – Flight No BA 361	Daily – Flight No BA 362	One-stop service
Malaysian Air	Boeing 757	Gatwick	Daily – Flight MA 407	Daily – Flight MA 408	Daylight flight
Southern Air	Boeing 747	Manchester	Mon, Tue, Thur, Fri, Sat	Tue, Wed, Fri, Sat, Sun	-

THIRD LEVEL
SPECIMEN
TUTORS

ASSIGNMENT 3 - Tutor's Input

Note to Tutors: Enter this text exactly as shown here, including formatting, page breaks and any deliberate errors. Save for use by candidates.

CHINA

General Information

Population:	1 billion
Area:	3,695,500 square miles
Currency:	Chinese Yuan

Distance from UK: 5053 miles

THIRD LEVEL
SPECIMEN
TUTORS

THIRD LEVEL
SPECIMEN
TUTORS

HEALTH REQUIREMENTS

The following vaccinations are recommended for all parts of China:

Polio
Typhoid
Yellow fever
Malaria
Hepatitis

THIRD LEVEL

THIRD LEVEL
SPECIMEN
TUTORS

ASSIGNMENT 3 - Marking Guide

KEY NOTES

CHINA

GENERAL INFORMATION

Population:	1 billion
Area:	3,695,500 square miles
Currency:	Chinese Yuan
	US$ readily accepted
Distance from UK:	5053 miles
Flying time:	10 hours
GMT:	+8 hours

CLIMATE

The climate in China varies considerably from place to place. As a guide the temperature in Beijing alone ranges from 2° C in January to over 31° C in July and August.

HEALTH REQUIREMENTS

The following vaccinations are recommended for all parts of China:

> Typhoid
> Polio
> Yellow Fever
> Malaria
> Hepatitis A

Travellers must ensure that they are in possession of the relevant vaccination certificates before undertaking their travel.

FLIGHTS

International flights in and out of Beijing are seldom affected by delay. Internal flights can be problematic, with unscheduled re-routing[1] and cancellation.

---

[1] The substitution of a flight with a ground alternative may be necessary.

15

THIRD LEVEL
SPECIMEN
TUTORS

MAIN SITES

We anticipate that most visitors will wish to visit four major sites:

BEIJING	Situated in the north, Beijing is a bustling city with several deluxe hotels. Visit the Forbidden City, the Summer Palace and the Ming Tombs. Just a short drive from Beijing is the Great Wall of China.
GUILIN	Located in the southern agricultural region, Guilin is justly famous for its spectacular landscapes of mountains and paddy fields. The Li River offers cruises to visitors.
SHANGHAI	Shanghai, one of China's greatest cities, is a bustling port offering exciting nightlife to tourists. The Grand Canal runs through the city. Visit the Bund, a busy waterfront boulevard, the Children's Palace and the Jade Buddha Temple.
XIAN	Xian is the site of the burial tomb of the Terracotta Warriors which were unearthed in the 1970s. Local excursions to hot springs and a Neolithic settlement are available from this location.

ITINERARIES

It is expected that travellers to China will be accompanied throughout their visit by a bilingual guide and will undertake a multi-centre holiday. A typical itinerary would be as follows:

Day 1	Fly from London Heathrow to Hong Kong
Day 2	Hong Kong
Day 3	Fly to Beijing
Days 4 and 5	Beijing including excursion to Great Wall of China
Day 6	Fly to Xian
Day 7	Xian - excursion to the Terracotta Warriors
Day 8	Fly to Shanghai
Days 9 and 10	Shanghai
Day 11	Fly to Guilin
Day 12	Guilin and surroundings
Day 13	Return to Beijing
Day 14	Fly to Hong Kong and onward flight to UK
Day 15	Arrive London Heathrow

As the number of travellers increases, so will the variety of itinerary be widened.

16

THIRD LEVEL
SPECIMEN
TUTORS

KEY NOTES

VISA INFORMATION

A full 10-year passport with at least 6 months' validity from the date of departure is required. A visa is also required[2]. A Visa Application Form and guidelines must be sent to all travellers on confirmation of their booking.

It is the responsibility of the traveller to ensure that all necessary documentation is acquired prior to departure.

BEST BUYS

There are many small outdoor markets in China in which items such as jade, antique ceramics, silk garments and wood, stone and bamboo carvings can be found. It is customary to bargain.

In the larger department stores, prices are fixed.

Stargazer Travel PLC
[Date]

---

[2] For travellers planning to visit China after Hong Kong, a visa must be acquired in the UK

17

THIRD LEVEL
SPECIMEN
TUTORS

ASSIGNMENT 4 - Marking Guide

WELCOME

Welcome to all our readers. This is only the second issue of Stargazer News but we have been delighted by the response to our first issue. Please keep us informed of current news from your branch. Send your information to Sally Webb at Head Office.

HOLIDAY COMPETITION

Mark Kennedy recently announced the winners of this year's competition. The first prize winner is Mrs Angela Betts of Chippenham. She'll be taking her husband Raymond with her when they travel to China for a 2-week holiday later this year.

NEW KEY NOTES

You should soon be in receipt of a new set of Key Notes. The topic is China. Please make sure that you read them carefully and retain them for future reference. We are hoping to expand our multi-centre holidays in China over the coming months. Special offers are in the pipeline. We'll keep you informed.

OPEN ALL HOURS

With effect from next week, Stargazer will be accessible on the Internet. Our website will give details of holiday destinations as well as examples of special travel offers. Let our customers know that they can contact us on www.stars.co.uk!

STAFF DEVELOPMENT

Any staff who wish to undertake training in a non-European language should contact Luisa de Valera at Head Office who will be happy to advise you.

CHEAPER TRAVEL INSURANCE

The introduction of our new annual travel insurance policy has proved to be very popular among our regular customers. It is by far the cheapest way to insure a family of four who typically take just two holidays a year. Rates start at only £58. New publicity leaflets are currently being prepared and will be delivered to your branches very soon.

ANNUAL STAFF GET-TOGETHER

This year it has been decided to organise a weekend in London instead of the usual Staff Dinner and Dance. The weekend will take place in late October and will include a staff dinner and a trip to a West End Show. Partners are welcome. The weekend will be free of charge to employees with a minimal charge to guests. Let Rob Atkins know if you wish to join us.

CONGRATULATIONS

Anna Jones of our Cardiff branch recently gave birth to twins. Many congratulations, Anna! We're looking forward to seeing you soon.

THIRD LEVEL
SPECIMEN
TUTORS

ASSIGNMENT 5 - Marking Guide

STARGAZER TRAVEL PLC

MINUTES OF THE MEETING of the Committee held on [date] at 1430 in the Conference
Room.

PRESENT   Mark Kennedy (Chairman)
                     Judy Grover (Secretary)
                     Sue Findlay
                     Robert Williams
                     Des Marchant
                     Luisa de Valera

1   APOLOGIES FOR ABSENCE

There were no apologies for absence.

2   MINUTES OF LAST MEETING

The Minutes of the last meeting were agreed and signed.

3   MATTERS ARISING

3.1   Mark Kennedy reported that shareholders were very pleased with recent performance and that plans for further expansion were a distinct possibility. He will report again following his meeting with the Board next week.

3.2   Des Marchant confirmed that Holidays Incorporated had gone into liquidation.

4   PRIZE COMPETITION

Sue Findlay reported that the winner of the Stargazer Holiday Competition was Mrs Angela Betts of Chippenham. Mrs Betts and her husband will travel to China for a 2-week break. A photocall was arranged with the local press.

Action: Sue Findlay

5   NEW DESTINATIONS

5.1   SOUTH AMERICA

Luisa de Valera commented that, owing to public demand for more exotic holidays, Peru and Chile were being investigated as possible new holiday destinations. Hotels were generally of good quality and able to offer lucrative discounts. Two-centre holidays were considered to be more attractive than tours or single-centre holidays.

Action: Luisa de Valera

THIRD LEVEL
SPECIMEN
TUTORS

5.2   JAPAN

Sue Findlay reported that last year more than 30 clients travelled to Japan for recreational purposes. Following discussion the Committee felt that exclusive package holidays to Japan might have limited success. It was agreed to contact the travellers and request their comments.

Action: Sue Findlay

6   FOREIGN LANGUAGE TRAINING

It was felt that foreign language skills amongst Head Office staff were sadly lacking. Faxes and telephone messages from overseas were often unintelligible owing to lack of linguistic knowledge. Mark Kennedy suggested that basic foreign language training should be made available to all staff as Staff Development. Luisa de Valera agreed to contact colleagues in the education sector.

Action: Luisa de Valera

7   ANY OTHER BUSINESS

There was no other business.

8   DATE AND TIME OF NEXT MEETING

Wednesday [date] at 1430.

Chairman ....   **Date** ....

ASSIGNMENT 6 - Marking Guide

STARGAZER TRAVEL INSURANCE

- MAKE SURE YOU'RE FULLY COVERED!

When arranging a holiday for yourself and your family, we know that you don't like to cut costs. You quite naturally want to treat your loved ones to a memorable experience ... and so a considerable length of time is spent planning your trip. But what about travel insurance? How much time do you spend on that? Our survey shows that the average traveller spends no more than 5 minutes organising insurance. So, is it any surprise that when claims are made, the results are often disappointing?

Think about an alternative ...

We at Stargazer Travel would like to tell you about our Annual Travel Insurance. It's an annual policy designed for individuals and families who travel abroad more than once a year. It is available for everyone under 70 years of age. Premiums can be paid monthly or annually by direct debit. The policy covers both business and holiday travel and there is no limit to the number of trips that can be taken during the one-year period. The only restriction relates to Winter Sports cover - one trip of up to 21 days' duration is permissible.

How much does it cost?

The Stargazer Annual Travel Insurance Policy costs only £60 per adult per year. Children between the ages of 2 and 15 years cost £26 each. Let's imagine a family of four who travel abroad twice a year (2 weeks in the Summer and a 1-week skiing holiday in the Winter).

Cost of premium = £60 + £60 + £26 + £26 = £172
Length of holiday = 21 days

Cost of cover = £172 ÷ 21 = £8.19 per day

We think that's a small price to pay for the satisfaction of knowing that your whole family is covered against accident, illness, loss of baggage, cancellation and personal liability.

What's more, the Winter Sports cover includes loss, theft or damage to equipment, cover against piste closure or avalanche and inability to ski due to illness or injury.

CONTACT YOUR STARGAZER TRAVEL AGENT NOW FOR AN APPLICATION FORM

Appendix 1: Key to exercises

EXERCISE 1.1

AIR TRAVEL

In the 1950s, air travel was a luxury which only the rich could afford. The average person would travel by train or by boat. Overseas travel was time-consuming and uncomfortable, and the traveller would arrive at his destination tired and dirty.

Nowadays most people travel by air. It is the fastest and easiest way to travel long distances. Most large cities have an airport within easy reach. Each year it becomes easier to buy a ticket, board an aeroplane and arrive at a faraway destination within hours of leaving home.

For long distances, it is often cheaper to travel by air.

Candidate's name

EXERCISE 1.2

FREEDOM HOLIDAYS
45-49 Charles Street
LEICESTER LE1 4JK

Date

Mrs S Robertson
2 The Square
LUTTERWORTH
LE9 2DF

Dear Mrs Robertson

Thank you for your letter requesting details of coach holidays to Spain and Portugal. I enclose a selection of brochures, which I hope you will find useful.

I should like to draw your attention to two holidays that are exceptionally good value. The first is a fly-drive holiday. A scheduled flight to Lisbon is followed by an 8-day coach tour around Portugal, with holiday-makers staying in traditional coaching inns. A detailed itinerary is included in the brochure. The all-inclusive price of £650 makes this holiday a real bargain.

The second is a 10-day coach tour around Southern Spain, with scheduled flights to and from Malaga. At only £750 per person, this is also excellent value for money.

Please let me know if you would like me to check availability on these holidays. I will need to know departure dates and the number of people travelling.

I look forward to hearing from you soon.

Yours sincerely

Tina George
Office Manager

Encs

EXERCISE 1.3

Thank you for choosing Comlon Contacts as your preferred booking agency. We offer a wide range of facilities, which range from restaurant and hotel bookings to large-scale corporate entertainment. We look forward to forging a long and successful business relationship with you.

Here are a few ideas for you to consider. Do you regularly take clients to lunch at top-class restaurants? We can arrange attractive discounts for you. Consult our comprehensive list of participating restaurants to see whether your favourite appears. When entertaining clients, we can also obtain tickets for all the leading West End shows at a fraction of the advertised price.

Want to know more? Give us a call on 0171 438 6521 now!

EXERCISE 1.4

This organisation is justly proud of its fine reputation. We employ approximately 300 members of staff within our company and this number increases during the summer months when we take on additional temporary staff.

If you would like to receive further information and an application form, please contact us immediately on extension 265. We shall be interviewing early in April and should be pleased to hear from you.

EXERCISE 2.1

**CRAVEN PARK SPORTS CENTRE
DAWLISH
SOUTH DEVON**

<u>SIMPLE RULES FOR A HEALTHY LIFESTYLE</u>

Eat three meals a day - with the emphasis on breakfast
(reduce saturated fat and meat)

Take a moderate amount of exercise!

Get a minimum of seven hours sleep a night

DO NOT SMOKE

Drink at least 2 litres of fresh water each day

Do not eat between meals

Keep your weight around the average for your height and build

Avoid unnecessary stressful situations

<u>BE HEALTHY AND BE HAPPY</u>

EXERCISE 2.2

<u>**SPECIAL OFFER!**</u>

DISCOVER MADRID

for only <u>£350</u> per person

Fly away to Spain this summer and visit one of Europe's
most attractive capital cities.

For only £350 per person you can enjoy

scheduled flights from your regional airport

3 nights' accommodation in a 4-star hotel

free buffet breakfast each day

free use of swimming pool and health club

free transfers to and from the airport in Madrid

free half-day coach tour of main tourist sights

To make your reservation or to obtain further details of this fantastic offer,
contact us on

0800 453 6921

Don't miss the chance to discover Spain's majestic capital!

HAPPY HOLIDAYS!

EXERCISE 2.3

FIVE GOOD REASONS WHY <u>YOU</u> SHOULD CHOOSE A COMLON CREDIT CARD ...

- ✓ low APR of just 6.5% plus no annual fee
- ✓ up to 56 days' interest-free credit if you pay your balance off in full each month
- ✓ choice of Visa or Mastercard
- ✓ accepted by 15 million outlets worldwide
- ✓ optional card protection cover

PLUS a £200 discount when you transfer the balance from your current card!

CAN YOU AFFORD TO TURN DOWN THIS FANTASTIC OFFER?

For further details, telephone us on 0800 962 534 now. We look forward to receiving your call.

EXERCISE 2.4

GODDINGTON PARK CONFERENCE CENTRE

Wilmington Lane
Nether Draycott
BS18 4JT

Tel: 01632 841298   Fax: 01632 841309

EXERCISE 2.5

<u>STAFF DEVELOPMENT NEWS</u>

Your Monthly Guide to Forthcoming Events

EXERCISE 3.1

<u>TRAVELLERS' WORLD</u>

We are pleased to announce the opening of our new

TRAVEL CLINIC

at

52 Sloane Street
LONDON EC4 2JR

<u>Telephone: 0171 349 8651</u>

We have a full range of vaccines in stock and give
practical advice on the prevention of tropical diseases

Mosquito nets, insect repellants and water-purifying kits
are also available at low cost

For **FREE** advice

call in and meet our professional staff
who will be delighted to help you

<u>No appointment necessary</u>

EXERCISE 3.2

COMLON DIRECT

INSURANCE WITH A DIFFERENCE!

At Comlon Direct, we constantly aim to improve the services we offer to our customers. We seek to offer you competitive rates with guaranteed monthly repayments so that you can plan ahead with confidence.

That's why we are pleased to announce our new personal loan for existing customers only. With an APR of only 11.5% this makes a Comlon Direct personal loan the cheapest on the market. So, if you're thinking of buying a new car, making those long-awaited home improvements or treating the family to an exotic holiday, this could be the opportunity that you've been waiting for!

Take a look at the enclosed table to see just how small your monthly repayments will be. Choose your own repayment period to suit your personal needs. Then simply complete the application form on page 4 and return it to Comlon Direct. We look forward to hearing from you soon.

EXERCISE 3.3

THREE STAR CONTRACT

Our Three Star Contract provides repair cover for all your gas systems and appliances and a yearly safety check which finds and repairs any faults. We provide this service to our customers for home systems only. Check your details carefully on the enclosed agreement.

> The price of your Three Star Contract is printed on the agreement form. You can pay by direct debit once a year or once a month, by credit or debit card or by a single payment each year for the year ahead. Whichever method of payment you choose, we will end the agreement if you miss any payment that is due.

Check the agreement now, add your signature and return it to us in the enclosed pre-paid envelope.

EXERCISE 3.4

OUR TEACHING STAFF

All our teachers are native speakers. They hold professional teaching qualifications and have had many years of teaching experience in the United Kingdom and overseas. Several have specialised in the study of linguistics and all are experts in the use of new technology to support language learning.

OUR COURSES

All our courses are designed to help you master the English language. You will have plenty of opportunity to listen, speak, read and write in your lessons. With only 12 students in each class, you can be sure of support and help from your teacher.

OUR CAMPUS

Located close to the main shopping streets of Central London, our campus is attractive and modern and our classrooms provide a pleasant learning environment. Three language laboratories support individual learning programmes and an open-access computer centre ensures that you have the opportunity to use modern software packages.

For further details of this year's courses and an application form, please contact Robert Goodman on 0800 345 871.

EXERCISE 3.5

WELCOME TO COMTECH INTERNATIONAL!

Each year millions of people undertake training to perfect their skills in the latest computer software packages. We at Comtech International pride ourselves on delivering courses of the highest standard to more than 20,000 students each year. Come and join us ....

OUR CAMPUS

Our campus is located in a quiet residential area just a short distance from Regent's Park. It comprises three attractive, modern buildings which house the teaching accommodation and the administration centre. A self-service restaurant and barbecue area overlook landscaped gardens. The local shopping area offers a wide range of amenities including bookshops, banks and a post office.

OUR TEACHING STAFF

Our team of teaching staff consists of highly qualified specialists who are not only experts in the latest software, but who have also attained professional teaching qualifications. Whatever you come to learn, you will be in very safe hands!

OUR COURSES

We offer a wide range of courses, ranging from a half-day introduction to computing to a programming course lasting for two weeks. You will find a full listing of our courses in our prospectus. However, if you require a course tailored to your own requirements, contact our Course Administrator and we can arrange an individualised course just for you.

Come and join us soon!
We look forward to hearing from you.

COMTECH INTERNATIONAL - TRAINING AT ITS BEST!

EXERCISE 4.1

PRICING POLICY

The prices quoted in this catalogue are those ruling at the time of printing. Due to circumstances beyond our control, prices may have to be altered up or down, including any alterations to the rate of purchase tax. The correct price will appear on your despatch note. If an item is not acceptable, it may be returned, providing it is sent back within 14 days and is in perfect condition.

All prices shown in this catalogue are cash prices. There is a service charge on extended credit accounts. Please contact your local agent for further details.

Homecare plc reserves the right to amend credit charges, to withdraw credit or, with prior written notice, to close an account.

EXERCISE 5.1

COMLON COMMUNICATIONS PLC

MINUTES of the Marketing Committee meeting which was held on (today's date) at 1100 in the Conference Room.

PRESENT   Susan Morris (Chairperson)
                  Usha Patel
                  Peter Francis
                  Antonio Varela

1   APOLOGIES FOR ABSENCE

Apologies were received from Jon Jefferson.

2   MINUTES OF LAST MEETING

The minutes of the last meeting were approved and signed.

3   MATTERS ARISING

There were no matters arising.

EXERCISE 5.2

SHORT COURSE PROGRAMME

CAREER AND PERSONAL DEVELOPMENT

The following courses will be held over the next three months. I shall be forwarding further details and exact dates to Section Leaders shortly. If you are interested in any of these courses, please contact Gita on Extension 246.

Course Title	Duration	Location
Assertiveness Training	1 day	Bristol
Presentation Skills	2 days	Head Office
Surviving Stress	1 day	Head Office
Team Building Techniques	2 days	Coventry
Time Management	1 day	Head Office
Using the Internet	1 day	Coventry

Please remember that a minimum of 15 participants is required for each course.

George Wallis
Personnel Manager

EXERCISE 5.3

GODDINGTON PARK CONFERENCE CENTRE

MEETING ROOM INFORMATION

Room Name	Palace	Stirling	Tamar	Wallace
Floor	Ground	Ground	First	First
Capacities				
theatre	130	35	45	50
classroom	70	20	20	25
boardroom	50	20	25	30
U-shape	50	18	18	24
lunch/dinner	-	-	-	-
reception	-	-	-	-
Dimensions				
length	13.29	7.63	9.15	9.76
width	11.74	7.93	9.15	9.76
area (sq m)	162	62	85.56	100
height	3.05	3.05	3.05	3.05

TECHNICAL INFORMATION

Room Name	Palace	Stirling	Tamar	Wallace
Floor	Ground	Ground	First	First
Lighting				
controls in room	yes	yes	yes	yes
dimmers	yes	no	yes	yes
blackout	yes	no	yes	yes
windows	yes	no	yes	yes
Sound	yes	yes	yes	yes
Power	40	10	10	6
Access				
door height	1.98	1.98	1.98	1.98
door width	2.36	0.81	0.81	1.22
Miscellaneous				
telephone points	yes	yes	yes	no
air conditioning	yes	no	no	no

Our conference accommodation is equipped with OHPs, screen, whiteboards, flipcharts, TV monitor, video recorder and slide carousel projectors.

EXERCISE 5.4

COMLON CONFERENCES PLC

MINUTES OF MEETING of the Committee held on [date] at 3.30 pm in Meeting Room A.

PRESENT   Stephen Knowles (Chairman)
                Alison Edgerley (Secretary)
                Yvonne Styles (Treasurer)
                Geeta Chana
                Pam Williamson
                Roz Charles
                Martin Davis

1   APOLOGIES FOR ABSENCE

Apologies were received from Jed Foster.

2   MINUTES OF LAST MEETING

The Minutes of the last meeting were agreed and signed.

3   MATTERS ARISING

3.1   Pam Williamson reported on negotiations with the Local Council regarding the widening of the main driveway. Copies of the correspondence were distributed to members.

3.2   Martin Davis read a letter from Voyager International, contracting to train all their new staff exclusively with Comlon. The estimated value of the work amounted to £150,000 per annum.

4   CURRICULUM DEVELOPMENT ISSUES

4.1   Roz Charles reported on the new modern language training modules currently being offered to local businesses at a reduced cost. These have proved to be very popular and a number of new companies have expressed interest. It was suggested that the range of languages should be extended as soon as possible.

Action: Roz Charles

4.2   Pam Williamson expressed concern over poor attendance on recent Time Management courses. It was agreed that the number of courses should be reduced in an effort to improve attendance figures.

Action: Pam Williamson

5   CAR PARKING

Members expressed concern about the restricted car parking currently available at the main site. On busy days, delegates encounter difficulty in parking and have on occasions had to park on the main road, causing complaints from local residents.

It was suggested that a new layout for the car park might avoid some problems. A new layout would be presented at the next meeting.

Action: Martin Davis

6   OPEN DAY

Yvonne Styles thanked all members for their valuable help in making last month's Open Day a great success. Over 250 representatives from local business and commerce attended and a significant amount of new work resulted from this chance to view the conference facilities.

A memo would be sent to all staff, both academic and administrative, to thank them for their efforts.

Action: Yvonne Styles

7   PUBLICITY

Concern was expressed about a new publicity campaign featuring a local training organisation. It was felt that this was detrimental to Comlon in that the publicity material suggested that the competitor was the only provider in the area. It was agreed to raise local awareness of Comlon by higher profile advertising.

Action: Stephen Knowles

8   DATE OF NEXT MEETING

To be advised.

Chairman ....   Date ....

2

EXERCISE 6.1

Part 1:

ENGLISH LANGUAGE CENTRE

Thank you for choosing the English Language Centre. The following information refers to our Junior courses:

You will receive 20 hours of lessons each week.

You will stay with an English family who will include you in family life.

Fees include breakfast and dinner on weekdays and full board at weekends.

Extra-curricular activities include outdoor sports and excursions to places of interest.

Part 2:

ENGLISH LANGUAGE CENTRE

Thank you for choosing the English Language Centre. The following information refers to our Adult courses:

You will receive 20 hours of lessons each week.

Your course will begin with an Entry Test which will take place at 9 am on the first day.

An optional examination will take place during the final week of the course.

Extra-curricular activities include visits to concerts and museums.

EXERCISE 6.2

JP/PS

Today's date

[Name]
[Address1]
[Address2]
[Address3]

Dear [Salutation]

Thank you for your cheque for [Amount], the final payment on your forthcoming holiday to [Destination]. I enclose your insurance policy document and a personalised itinerary.

Your travel tickets will be forwarded to your home address approximately 14 days prior to your departure date. Please check that the names on the tickets are correct.

On behalf of Comlon Holidays we hope you have an enjoyable holiday.

Yours sincerely

Jan Percival
Reservations Manager

Encs

EXERCISE 6.3

176

Name	Address1	Address2	Address3	Salutation	Amount	Destination
Miss Rita Lewis	15 High Street	COVENTRY	CV2 8LP	Miss Lewis	£1500	Australia
Mr John Byrne	6 Walnut Close	NOTTINGHAM	NG3 9RV	Mr Byrne	£800	Denmark
Mrs Sarah Day	3 The Avenue	WIGSTON	LE6 2MN	Mrs Day	£1950	Malaysia

EXERCISE 6.4

COMLON BOOKS

Welcome to Comlon Books - a unique book club that always gives you, the reader, the freedom to choose the books you want, when you want them. We offer high quality books at reduced prices, often as much as 50% less than the recommended retail price. Not only that, if you are not delighted with your choice, we offer a unique service which enables you to return the book for a full refund.

HOW THE CLUB WORKS

Each month we will send you our Comlon Newsletter which gives details of the titles currently available for sale. A review accompanies each listing. All books have been especially selected by our editorial team to ensure that you have access to some of the best writers and their works.

YOUR COMMITMENT

All we ask of our members is that they purchase 3 books within the first 12 months of membership. All books featured will be at a reduced price. Each month an order form will accompany the Comlon Newsletter. You should make your choice and place your order within 10 days of receipt of the Newsletter. Your books will be delivered within 48 hours.

PAYMENT

Payment can be made by cheque or credit card. Payment should accompany each order. In the unlikely case of a book being returned to us, we will credit your account immediately. All payments and credits will be shown on your monthly statement.

DATA PROTECTION ACT

Comlon Books always operates within the terms and spirit of the Data Protection Act. We are registered with the Data Protection Registrar. Occasionally we make lists of members' names and addresses available to companies whose products or services we feel may be of interest. Please let us know if you do not wish to receive such mailings.

HAPPY READING!

EXERCISE 7.1

COMLON TRAINING PLC

APPLICATION FORM

Please complete and return this form to Comlon Training PLC, Warwick Chambers, Granby Place, Leicester LE6 4HP.

DELEGATE DETAILS

Full Name ....

Home Address ....

....

Postcode .... Telephone ....

COMPANY DETAILS

Company Name ....

Address ....

.... Postcode ....

Telephone .... Fax ....

COURSE DETAILS

Course Title ....

Preferred Dates   (1) ....

                   (2) ....

                   (3) ....

I enclose a cheque for £50 made payable to Comlon Training PLC. I understand that this deposit is refundable only in the event of the course being cancelled.

SIGNATURE .... DATE ....

EXERCISE 7.2

ESSENTIAL CONFERENCE INFORMATION

OUR AIM

Our aim is to provide you with all you need to make your event a success. Let us know how we can help you.

LOCATION

Goddington Park is situated in beautiful countryside only 10 miles from the centre of Bristol. Easily accessible by road, rail and air, it is an attractive location for meetings and conferences.

CONFERENCE FACILITIES

Goddington Park is the ideal choice for management training or business meetings - in whatever form they take - conferences, seminars or workshops. We can accommodate half-day, full-day and weekend functions. Just let us know your particular requirements.

We have four well-equipped training and meeting rooms which can accommodate up to 40 delegates in theatre-style seating. Smaller groups are catered for in our syndicate rooms which can comfortably seat up to 12 delegates in each.

Each meeting room is equipped with television, video, overhead projector and flip chart. Desktop projection equipment is available on request.

RESIDENTIAL FACILITIES

Goddington Park is a residential centre offering all the comforts and benefits of a country house. There are 25 study bedrooms located on the first and second floors. All have their own distinctive character and most overlook the gardens. A lift serves both floors.

Each room has a private bathroom with shower, wc and washbasin. There is a television and a hair dryer in each room. Tea and coffee-making facilities are also provided.

FOOD AND DRINK

A large, airy restaurant overlooking the gardens is open to delegates throughout their stay. Our resident chef can offer a wide range of menu options. Let us know your preferences in advance and we will be pleased to supply you with sample menus.

RELAXATION

To relax after a busy day, Goddington Park offers a range of activities - croquet, tennis, table-tennis, billiards and even a fitness suite with exercise equipment. A small indoor swimming pool aids relaxation.

EXERCISE 7.3

STRESS AT WORK

The workplace is generally acknowledged to be one of the major sources of stress for many people. As most of us spend more time at work than we do at home, it is inevitable that difficult working conditions can lead to feelings of stress.

However, work also offers many opportunities to channel stress towards positive ends. A stimulating and challenging job can provide the means by which an individual can forget about problems in other areas of life.

Change and Uncertainty

Much stress is brought about by changes in the workplace. A merger or take-over, a major reorganisation, changing work patterns - all of these can cause employees to suffer from stress. It is the feeling of insecurity that fuels the stress and this is often made worse by poor communication.

External Pressures

Many jobs are directly subjected to external pressures - meeting an urgent order, making a presentation to a major client, dealing with the general public - and an individual can experience strong feelings of insecurity on a daily basis.

Environmental Stress

Many employees work in a stressful environment, where poor light, inadequate ventilation, overcrowding, poor security and drab surroundings often combine to depress even the most optimistic worker. The company is duty-bound by law[1] to ensure that basic standards are met and employees should draw problems to the attention of management.

---

[1] The Health and Safety at Work Act 1974

1

SOME SOLUTIONS

Here are some suggestions which might improve the stress at work:

Communication

Ordinary work problems will be defused if you can talk about them. Try to involve your family, trustworthy colleagues and friends and acquaintances who work in similar jobs. In this way potentially stressful situations can be avoided. Ideally, you should aim to talk directly to your line manager.

Forward Planning

Whilst all stressful situations cannot be avoided, sensible forward planning can ensure that you are not forced into last-minute actions. Use checklists for regular events, prepare well in advance of meetings and try to use your time effectively.

Feedback

Try to make sure that you receive regular feedback on your performance from the person to whom you are answerable. In this way you will be alerted before any minor concerns become major issues.

Physical Conditions

Do all you can to make sure that your personal working environment is comfortable and efficient. If you work at a desk or computer, check that your seating is suitable[2], that your VDU is glare-free and that you have adequate space in which to perform your job.

By making a few simple changes to your work patterns, you will find that you can eliminate some stress from your working life.

---

[2] Display Screen Equipment Regulations 1992

2

Appendix 2: Advice for students taking LCCIEB practical examinations

Before starting your studies

1 Choose a school, college or private teacher who is familiar with the LCCIEB Practical Word Processing assessment scheme and who has a reputation for good results.

2 Attend your lessons regularly and practise as often as you can.

3 Look carefully at the syllabus. Check that the hardware and/or software that you are using is capable of performing all the functions to be tested. As you make progress, tick off the functions you have learned.

4 If you intend to take the assignments for Second or Third Level Practical Word Processing, remember that you will also be tested on the functions required for the lower levels.

5 Try to work through some past assignments. This will help you to become familiar with the layout, content and difficulty of the assignments at each level. There are individual exercises in this book which test specific functions. At the end of the book you will also find sets of assignments and marking copies at First, Second and Third Levels. Check your work carefully against the marking copy and learn from your mistakes.

6 When you are confident that you can successfully undertake all functions at a particular level, speak to your tutor about entering for the Practical Word Processing assignments. He or she will advise you whether you are ready for assessment.

7 Remember that the assignments must be completed within the stated time allowance. You must practise under time-constrained conditions.

8 It is your responsibility to make sure that you have been entered for the assessment, even if the entry is organised by your tutor or the college.

Before the assessment

1 Make sure that you know when and where the assessment will take place. Arrive in good time and check that the equipment you are using is working effectively. In particular, check that the printer is working and that the print-outs are clear and legible.

2   Check that you have everything that you will need. You will need a pencil, a ruler and (if you wish to use one) a dictionary. Don't forget your glasses if you use them!

The assignments

1   Each assignment is given a time allowance. Some asignments must be completed within 30 minutes; others must be completed within 60 minutes. Use your time sensibly: always spend time reading through the assignment before you begin; allow time at the end to check your work carefully before handing it to your tutor for marking.

2   Save your work regularly. Give each assignment an appropriate file name. Use a file name that you can easily find again. Sometimes you will be asked to retrieve a file which has been keyed in by your tutor in advance. It is a good idea to save the amended document under the same file name in your own directory.

3   Check your work carefully, since each inaccuracy counts as an error. You may use the computer's spellchecker if you wish, but always check your work personally, by reading it, as well.

4   Make sure that your name appears on every assignment.

5   Follow all instructions carefully. It is a good idea to tick each instruction as it is completed. Each instruction overlooked will result in a penalty.

6   For Second and Third Level assignments, you will be required to expand abbreviations. Make sure that you are familiar with the list of abbreviations. You may not use the list during assessment.

7   Try to display your work as attractively as possible. Always include a date on letters and memoranda. The easiest way to display correspondence is by using the fully blocked style with open punctuation.

8   You must produce a print-out of every assignment for marking. At First Level, all assignments will fit comfortably on to one sheet of A4 paper. At Second and Third Levels, however, multi-page documents are required.

Finally, I hope that you will be a successful candidate. If you work through this book systematically and practise the exercises, you will soon learn what is needed for success in Practical Word Processing.

Good luck!

Index

Note: Exercise and figure numbers are given in bold print.